THE
RATIONALITY
OF BELIEF
IN
GOD

CENTRAL ISSUES IN PHILOSOPHY SERIES

BARUCH A. BRODY
series editor

~~~~~~

Baruch A. Brody
MORAL RULES AND PARTICULAR CIRCUMSTANCES

Hugo A. Bedau
JUSTICE AND EQUALITY

Mark Levensky
HUMAN FACTUAL KNOWLEDGE

George I. Mavrodes
THE RATIONALITY OF BELIEF IN GOD

Robert Sleigh
NECESSARY TRUTH

David M. Rosenthal
THE MENTAL AND THE PHYSICAL

Richard Grandy
THEORIES AND OBSERVATIONS IN SCIENCE

Gerald Dworkin
DETERMINISM, FREE WILL, AND MORAL RESPONSIBILITY

David P. Gauthier
MORALITY AND RATIONAL SELF-INTEREST

Charles Landesman
THE FOUNDATIONS OF KNOWLEDGE

Adrienne and Keith Lehrer
THE THEORY OF MEANING

edited by

GEORGE I. MAVRODES
University of Michigan

THE
RATIONALITY
OF BELIEF
IN
GOD

Prentice-Hall, Inc., Englewood Cliffs, New Jersey

Library of Congress Catalog Card Number: 79-117010

Printed in the United States of America

C 13–753194–X
P 13–753186–9

Current Printing (last number):

10 9 8 7 6 5 4 3 2

PRENTICE-HALL INTERNATIONAL, INC., London
PRENTICE-HALL OF AUSTRALIA, PTY. LTD., Sydney
PRENTICE-HALL OF CANADA, LTD., Toronto
PRENTICE-HALL OF INDIA PRIVATE LIMITED, New Delhi
PRENTICE-HALL OF JAPAN, INC., Tokyo

Foreword

The Central Issues in Philosophy series is based upon the conviction that the best way to teach philosophy to introductory students
is to experience or to *do* philosophy with them. The basic unit of
philosophical investigation is the particular problem, and not the
area or the historical figure. Therefore, this series consists of sets of
readings organised around well-defined, manageable problems. All
other things being equal, problems that are of interest and relevance
to the student have been chosen.

Each volume contains an introduction that clearly defines the
problem and sets out the alternative positions that have been taken.
The selections are chosen and arranged in such a way as to take the
student through the dialectic of the problem; each reading, besides
presenting a particular point of view, criticizes the points of view
set out earlier.

Although no attempt has been made to introduce the student in
a systematic way to the history of philosophy, classical selections
relevant to the development of the problem have been included. As
a side benefit, the student will therefore come to see the continuity,
as well as the breaks, between classical and contemporary thought.
But in no case will a selection be included merely for its historical
significance; clarity of expression and systematic significance are the
main criteria for selection.

BARUCH A. BRODY

94608

Contents

*THE
RATIONALITY
OF BELIEF
IN
GOD*

Introduction

I. GENERAL REMARKS

PURPOSE AND STRUCTURE OF THIS BOOK   This book is intended as a brief introduction to the philosophy of religion for readers who have had little or no formal study of philosophy. The subject matter, of course, constitutes a vast field. But since this book will probably be used mainly in college courses where only a few weeks will be devoted to the philosophy of religion, it was necessary to keep it rather short. I have therefore restricted it to a single topic, and even this topic is treated very briefly. But I hope that it will provide a suggestion of the philosophical thinking in this area.

The main body of the book consists of selections from the writings of a number of outstanding thinkers from the fourteenth to the twentieth century. The authors include devout believers, vigorous atheists, and some who fall between these extremes. The views expressed are correspondingly diverse. Therefore, the reader who comes to this book with the expectation that he will find in it a single consistent answer to his religious questions will be disappointed. It is a mistake to suppose that for any profound and important question we can simply take over someone else's answer without thought and struggle of our own. For the reader who is prepared to begin, or to continue, the process of working out an answer I hope that this book may provide some stimulation.

This introductory essay provides a context in which to consider the reprinted selections. The reader should test the essay as he reads, just as he would a classroom lecture, retaining only what he considers good.

THE QUESTIONS DISCUSSED   I have tried to select readings about belief in God which concern similar questions. It is difficult to formulate precisely what these questions are and what they have in common, but the following list should give the reader some idea of the problems treated.

Critical questions
1. Is belief in God rational?
2. Ought a person to believe in God?
3. Is belief in God justified?
4. If a person were to believe in God would he damage his intellectual integrity?

All of the authors represented here are dealing in some way with this group of questions. In the remainder of this essay I will refer to all of these questions as questions about the *rationality* of belief in God. But in using that terminology for convenience I do not intend to prevent the reader from making useful distinctions among these questions. In the remainder of the essay I have grouped the responses of these authors into several categories and provided some introduction which may both aid and provoke the reader as he proceeds to the selections themselves.

II. PROOF

A. Preliminary Considerations

PROOF AND RATIONALITY   One suggestion often made is that a person's belief in God would be rational if there were a proof of God's existence. Perhaps a better statement of this suggestion is that a person's belief in God would be rational if he *had* a proof of God's existence. For it is hard to see how the mere existence of a proof (whatever that might mean) could make a person's belief rational unless he somehow possessed that proof. Unfortunately this distinction has frequently been overlooked, so that whereas there has been much discussion of theistic proofs, there has been little discussion of what it would be for a person to have one of these as the ground of the rationality of his belief. One way in which a proof might function as such a ground is mentioned below.

In any case, this suggestion (in either of the forms mentioned above) should be sharply distinguished from the claim that a person's belief is rational *only if* he has a proof of God's existence. For this latter claim excludes, as the former does not, the possibility that there may be other grounds for rational belief. It would be rash to exclude this possibility, at least at the outset. Nevertheless, despite these other possible grounds for rational belief (several of which are discussed below and represented by selections in this book), most western philosophers who have wanted to defend the rationality of theistic belief have tried to do so by formulating and defending proofs of God's existence. Consequently, a large proportion of the criticisms of theistic belief has also centered around proofs. This aspect of the topic has therefore loomed very large, perhaps disproportionately large, in philosopher's discussions of religion.

DISCURSIVE PROOFS Most philosophers who have discussed theistic proofs have limited themselves mainly to a consideration of discursive types of proof. A discursive proof is one which is given entirely by means of discourse, that is, by talking or writing. It consists entirely of an argument, that is, of one or more statements which are premises and a statement which is the conclusion. In common speech, of course, we use the word "prove" more broadly. For example, a person may prove that he can swim not by asserting premises and conclusions, perhaps not by asserting anything at all, but by actually swimming a few lengths of the pool. If there are theological analogues of this latter type of proof they probably belong in the section on experience, below. In this section I will consider discursive proofs only.

A further distinction is often drawn between *deductive* and *inductive* proofs or arguments. The former are those in which the premises apparently provide conclusive evidence for the conclusion, whereas in the latter the premises provide only some probability in favor of the conclusion. Most philosophers in this field have defended or criticized deductive proofs, although a few have cast their arguments—especially those of the teleological type—in the inductive form. And occasionally it is not clear which type is intended.

POSITIVE CRITERIA FOR PROOF   Not every attempted proof is a "good" one. Some fail to measure up to appropriate standards. Two positive criteria for proof have been widely recognized by philosophers. I would like to suggest a third which should be added to the list. The first generally recognized criterion is that of validity. This criterion refers to the *construction* of the argument, to the way in which the premises are related to each other and to the conclusion. (The detailed study of the ways in which statements may be related to each other is, of course, a large part of the subject matter of logic.) An argument is valid only if it would be impossible for the conclusion to be false if the premises were true. In a sense, the truth of the premises in a valid argument is binding upon the truth of the conclusion.

It is important to notice two facts in connection with this first criterion, however. First, if the conclusion is true it does not follow that the argument is valid. For the conclusion may be true even though its truth is not supported by the premises. Second, if one or more premises are false it does not follow that the argument is invalid. For even though the premises are in fact false they may be logically related to the conclusion in such a way that *if* they were true then the conclusion would have to be true also. Therefore the validity of an argument in no way guarantees the truth of its conclusion. Validity, though necessary for a good argument, is by no means a sufficient condition.

At this point it may be worth suggesting that clarity of discussion could be improved if the term "logical" were restricted to matters of logic, rather than applied vaguely as a general commendation of arguments, ideas, decisions, actions, and so forth. That an argument was logical would then mean, presumably, that it was valid. And, as we noted above, this would not guarantee that the argument provided any support for its conclusion. (If "logical" were restricted in this way it would have no immediately apparent application to ideas, beliefs, or actions. Of course, a person who wished to apply it to such things could specify a second sense which it was to bear in such applications.)

The second criterion for a satisfactory argument is that all of its premises should be true. If both of these criteria are satisfied, then, of course, the conclusion of the argument must also be true. Arguments which satisfy both of these criteria are usually said to be *sound*.

Although the soundness of an argument guarantees that its conclusion is true, it does not guarantee that anyone's belief in that conclusion is rational. Here we return to the distinction between there *being* a proof of God's existence and someone's *having* such proof. I suggest that we should recognize a third criterion which must be satisfied if a proof is to render a belief rational: The person involved must have a rational belief that the proof is sound. Unless a person has faith in God, the mere fact that there is a sound argument for God's existence—or even that he has heard such an argument—cannot make his belief in God rational. But if there is in fact a sound proof, *and if he has a rational belief that it is sound*, then he will also be entitled to a rational belief in its conclusion.

I suggest that these three, positive criteria, then, can be used in assessing the adequacy of proofs.

CRITICIZING A PROOF   If the above criteria are necessary for a satisfactory proof, then an attempted proof may be criticized by arguing (or, perhaps less persuasively, by merely claiming) that it fails to satisfy one or more of them. Most criticisms of theistic arguments concentrate on the first two criteria. Of course such criticisms may sometimes be correct. But it is worthwhile to ask ourselves while reading criticisms whether (assuming that he is sincere) the critic is entitled to more than a claim that the argument fails to satisfy the third criterion (relative to the critic).

Another way of putting the point is this: When a person seriously proposes and defends an argument, then—if he is speaking in good faith—we may assume he is claiming that it is logically valid and that its premises are true. That is, he commits himself; he "sticks his neck out" about the logic and about the facts alleged by the premises. To stick your neck out in that way, to run that risk of being wrong, is part of good-faith argumentation. A person who is unsure of his position and unwilling to run a risk about logic and fact cannot in good faith propose or defend his argument. If an argument is proposed, however, and a critic wishes to attack its validity or the truth of its premises, then *that critic must also be willing to stick his neck out*. To claim that a certain argument is invalid requires as strong a commitment on matters of logic as to claim that it is valid. To maintain that a given premise is false is to make a commitment about the fact alleged. If a prospective critic finds himself unwilling to run that risk of being wrong, then he cannot properly challenge the truth or validity claimed for the argument. And if he does challenge the argument his reader has every right to ask upon what basis he is making his commitments. In controversies over philosophical arguments the critic and the defender of the argument meet on equal ground. Neither of them should be accorded a privileged sanctuary, immune from probing.

A critic may content himself, however, with the weaker claim that *he does not believe* that the argument is valid or that its premises are true. Unless he is obviously insincere, there is no point in challenging him on this claim. And his claim, if sincere, does demonstrate that the argument which he criticizes in this way is not adequate to provide *him* with a rational belief. Whether that argument is adequate to provide us (or anyone else) with such a belief remains, of course, an open question.

If an argument is sound its conclusion is true. If it is unsound, however, we can make no assumptions about its conclusion. The conclusions of such arguments are just as likely to be true as to be false; every statement, true as well as false, can be made the conclusion of innumerable unsound arguments. It would therefore be a mistake to base any judgment about the truth of a statement upon the unsoundness of an argument of which that statement happens to be the conclusion.

B. Types of Theistic Proof

TYPES AND PARTICULAR PROOFS Theistic proofs are often divided into several categories. The most common of these schemes distinguishes ontological, cosmological, teleological, and moral proofs; these are the categories which I will discuss below. But we should realize that neither this scheme nor any other similar classificatory scheme can be made precise. I, at least, do not know a way of drawing the lines sharply between most of the categories. It is always possible that we may find an argument which we cannot fit easily into this scheme. But for many of the best known and most widely discussed arguments this scheme provides a useful preliminary method of categorizing them.

We would do well to avoid, however, a danger associated with this scheme. Some people, including some professional philosophers who should be more careful, speak of "the ontological argument," "the teleological argument," and so forth, as if there were some *one* argument which was the ontological or teleological argument. And they may then make some judgment about it, for example that it is sound. This practice is highly misleading, since a large number of arguments differing from each other in various ways, have in fact gone under each of these names. Any thinker is free to invent a new member of one of these classes at any time. Each of these categories constitutes something like a family of arguments which resemble each other in certain important ways and differ in other ways. And just as in human families it is possible for one member to be a scoundrel and another a reliable man, so it is possible that some members of one such argument family should be valid and others invalid, and some might use true premises and others false ones. Unless we found some positive reason for doing otherwise, we would probably be wiser to use this scheme mainly as a convenient sorting device, while remembering that it is the various particular arguments, and not the families to which they belong, which have most of the crucial virtues and faults.

In an attempt to keep this point before us, I shall refer to these categories as *argument types*.

ONTOLOGICAL TYPE ARGUMENTS   The common feature distinguishing arguments of this type from others is also the feature which makes them the most puzzling. It is that the premises of such arguments seem to include nothing beyond one or more definitions or the analysis of one or more concepts or ideas. In contrast with other types of theistic arguments, the premises of ontological type arguments appear to say nothing at all about the world.

The term or concept most often analyzed is *God*, though in some forms of this argument type the concept analyzed may be one like *perfection* or *greatness*. In every case the conclusion drawn is that some entity corresponding to the analyzed term really exists. This attempt to derive a conclusion about real existence from nothing more than a definition or a piece of conceptual analysis strikes most readers, at least at first, as a sleight-of-hand. They think something must be wrong with it, and they may be right. Perhaps no argument of this general structure can be sound. This has been the view of most philosophers, including many who believed in God on other grounds. And yet arguments of this type have had very eminent defenders, including some contemporary philosophers. It has proved extraordinarily difficult to make clear what fault there is, if any, in the best formulations of ontological arguments.

Critics have most often asserted that there is something illicit about including any reference to existence in a definition, or in supposing that existence or anything which implies existence can be part of the content of any concept or idea. This view is often associated with the slogan that "existence is not a predicate." But, of course, defenders of this argument type claim that existence *is* an integral element in at least one concept and the critics have not clearly given any persuasive reason for their denial. The reader whose interest is aroused by this type of argument should consult the bibliography for further material, since the argument is too subtle to be followed further effectively in the space available here.

Probably the most famous, and one of the best of logical-type formulations is that of Anselm, reprinted below. (It is worth noting that some of Anselm's strongest contemporary defenders hold that his best formulation appears not in the first reprinted section, but in the second and third and in his reply to his critic.) A criticism by Gaunilon (a contemporary of Anselm), which anticipates many later responses, is included together with portions of Anselm's reply. Another critique of this type of argument appears in the paper by J. J. C. Smart.

COSMOLOGICAL TYPE ARGUMENTS   Arguments of this type and the two types discussed below all begin with some premise about the world. In arguments of the cosmological type (the name is derived from a Greek word meaning "universe") this premise refers to some very general fact about the world. The truth of these premises has rarely been questioned. St. Thomas Aquinas' famous "five ways," reprinted below, include brief formulations of three versions of this type. In the first one the initial premise is that some things in the world move, or, more properly, undergo change. The second version parallels the first very closely, but begins with the premise that there are some cases of cause and effect. The third begins with the most general fact of all—that some things exist even though, considered in themselves, it is possible for them not to exist. This fact is sometimes described by saying that *contingent* things exist, or that the world is contingent.

From these premises Thomas professes to deduce the existence of a "first mover," a "first cause," and a "being having of itself its own necessity." In a later section of the *Summa Theologica* he presents arguments intended to show that these terms refer to the same being, the being intended by the word "God," at least as it is used in the Christian sense. But the deduction is not made from these premises alone. Most importantly, in each of the arguments a similar premise appears, presumably a general principle of some sort, to the effect that an infinite series of a certain kind is impossible. There has been some difficulty in understanding clearly just what this principle is, that is, what kind of series Thomas thinks is impossible, as well as in determining whether the principle is true. The reader is referred to the careful treatment of these arguments in F. C. Copleston's account, reprinted below, and to Smart's criticism. In addition, the first part of A. E. Taylor's paper presents a somewhat different version of this type of argument, related to Thomas' first way and focused on the idea of *explaining* natural phenomena. His line of argument, too, requires that a set of explanations, to be satisfactory, must not simply be endless. Besides these discussions, of course, there have been many others in philosophical literature. The bibliography refers to a few of these which will in turn provide references to others.

TELEOLOGICAL TYPE ARGUMENTS   The name of this type of argument is derived from a Greek word meaning "goal" or "purpose"; these arguments begin with a premise to the effect that some part of the world (or perhaps the whole world) appears to be designed in such a way as to accomplish a certain purpose. Thomas' fifth argument is of this type. As he reminds us, we know why it is that arrows do not fly off randomly in all directions but generally land near the target. It is because they are so aimed by human beings with purposes and will. But there are many natural entities and processes which similarly exhibit a lack of randomness and an apparent goal-directedness. Must they not also be directed by a purpose and a will, that of the designer of the world?

Many versions of this argument type have focused attention on some of the incredibly complex and finely adjusted mechanisms exhibited by living organisms, for these are probably the most striking, at least initially, of the world's instances of apparent design. To some extent the rise of evolutionary theories may have weakened the force of these considerations, though we should not be too hasty in assuming that this weakening was justified. The mere discovery of a mechanism which produces items of apparent design does not of itself militate against the view that a designing mind is at work. A person may initially think that a wristwatch is so complex and purposive an object that it must have been made by a human craftsman. It is conceivable, however, that watches could be produced in a completely automated factory with no human intervention and that our hypothetical person could be convinced of this. But it does not follow that he should therefore give up his interest in the designer. For if he thought a watch was wonderful, what must he think of the factory which produces watches? Must it not suggest a designer even more forcefully?

Some recent thinkers, therefore, have sought to include evolutionary theories explicitly within the teleological type of argument and in this way to provide it with a broader base. F. R. Tennant (see bibliography) has focused attention on large-scale features of the universe, its adaptability to life, the persistent evolutionary development of more complex nervous systems up to the appearance of man, the adaptability of the world for the development of moral and esthetic consciousness, and so forth. Rather than being completely negative, evolutionary theories thus may have some positive significance for arguments of this type.

A number of persuasive criticisms have been leveled against the teleological type of argument. For one thing, improbable things may happen by chance and, in fact, may be *likely* to happen if the number of "trials" is large enough. Indeed, any event which could happen in the world or any state in which the world could exist is highly improbable when compared to the vast number of other events or states which could have replaced it. But it may not be unlikely that *some* of these events or states should occur. (For example, it is highly unlikely that someone will be dealt thirteen spades in his next bridge hand. Whatever mundane assortment of cards he does receive, however, is just as unlikely as thirteen spades. Yet such hands are dealt all the time without stacking the deck.) Therefore some doubt may arise about versions of this argument which rely heavily upon the prior improbability of a world such as ours.

Another criticism sometimes made is that the procedure of the teleologist is somewhat circular. He cannot proceed from a prior knowledge of what kind of world God would design to the conclusion that, since the world *is* of this kind, it must have been designed by God. He has rather to discover the purpose of the world by observing what the world does; he then concludes that it is designed by observing that it does things conducive to that purpose!

These objections and some others cited in the paper by Smart seem to have some force. The final assessment, of course, must be made by each individual for himself.

MORAL TYPE ARGUMENTS   These arguments characteristically contain statements about morality as premises. In general, they argue that some moral fact could not be as it is, or that the moral life would make no sense, or that we could not have moral obligations, and so forth, if there were no God. There is a hint of this type of argument in Thomas' fourth way, but it is not worked out in any detail. Two other examples of this kind of argumentation are included below. One is that of Kant, who rejects the previously mentioned types of proof as defective. He has previously argued that there is an absolute moral law which is binding upon every man just because he is a rational being, and he believes that a man can know there is such a law and discover what its structure is regardless of what he thinks about God. But he also believes that part of our moral obligation involves striving to attain the highest good (*summum bonum*) and perhaps helping others to attain it. In the section reprinted below he maintains that the highest good consists of a combination of morality and of happiness proportional to morality. Being moral is our business and no one can do it for us. But it is not possible for us to bring about our own happiness in proportion to our moral worthiness, for we do not control the circumstances of our lives. Only a God who controlled the world could bring about that part of the highest good. Kant thinks it would make no sense to suppose that we have an obligation to strive for the highest good unless its achievement were a real possibility. Therefore, he concludes, since we do have such an obligation God must exist. (He argues similarly that we must be immortal since we cannot achieve the highest good in this life.)

A peculiarity of Kant's view not characteristic of arguments of this kind is his assertion on other grounds that there can be no *theoretical* knowledge of God, since he limited such knowledge to subject matter that can be apprehended in sense perception and to knowledge about the structure of the rational mind. He therefore calls the conclusion of his moral argument a *practical postulate,* that is, something which we must believe if the demands of morality are to make sense for our practical life. But since he is convinced that these demands do make sense and are quite objective and binding, it is not easy to see the real value of this distinction.

A somewhat different kind of moral argument is presented in the second part of Taylor's paper, in a form closer to the suggestions in Thomas' fourth way. Taylor argues that our moral obligations often require the sacrifice of some real good, a sacrifice which is justified only if some greater good is achieved or preserved thereby. In some of these cases one temporal, "worldly" good is sacrificed for some greater temporal good. But, Taylor says, there is no temporal good which we may not be called upon to sacrifice at some time or other. There must therefore be some transtemporal, transworldly good which exceeds all others and justifies such sacrifices. And this good, he suggests, is God.

Moral type arguments are often attacked on their premises. Someone may deny, for example, that we ever have the sort of obligation which Taylor discusses. Taylor's argument does not prove that we do have this sort of obligation, but this absence of proof is not a special weakness of the argument. For no argument (unless it is circular) contains a proof of its own premises. Another argument, of course, might have that premise as its conclusion, but this argument would in turn contain its own unproved premises. *The attempt to prove everything by argument simply leads to an infinite regress of arguments.* This procedure is pointless. If we are going to use argumentation in good faith, then we must be willing to begin with what we already know (or think we know) and to proceed from there. A reader confronted with an attack against the premise of a moral type argument (or, for that matter, of any other argument) must ask himself whether he himself is prepared to deny its truth. If so, he will be prepared to agree with the attack. If, however, he is prepared neither to deny nor to assert the truth of that premise, then he can only report the argument's ineffectiveness *for him.* (Of course, if he finds himself in agreement with the premise then he should consider seriously the remainder of the argument.) Taylor believes that a person who reflects on his own experience of moral obligation and the moral life—if that person "really cares" about morality—will discover in his experience the truth of the premise with which he begins. The reader who is interested must, of course, undertake this reflection for himself.

ANTITHEISTIC ARGUMENTS Most of those who have rejected belief in God and who have been interested in argumentation upon the subject have contented themselves with attempts to refute arguments in favor of God's existence. But there has also been substantial interest in positive arguments which reach the conclusion that there is no God. Most of these fall into two classes. The first is somewhat analogous to the ontological type of argument. This class does not rely upon any fact about the world, even the most general, but rather maintains that there is something logically incoherent within the very concept of *God* itself, so that nothing could possibly exist corresponding to that concept. Although this line of argumentation has obvious affinities with that, say, of Anselm, it is not as puzzling or as initially implausible as Anselm's. For the claim that nothing can exist corresponding to a self-contradictory concept appears more straightforward and plausible than the claim that there is a concept to which some real existent *must* correspond. In this sense, logical defects seem, at least at first, to be more relevant to existence than do logical virtues. Critics of this kind of argumentation have usually replied that the concept of God is not self-contradictory and that some logical mistake is made by those who suppose that it is.

Although no example of this kind of argument is reprinted below, one of the most interesting recent attempts at it, that by J. N. Findlay, is cited in the bibliography.

The more common and influential type of antitheistic argument is analogous to the teleological and moral types of argument; in fact, it is often advanced not as an independent antitheistic proof but as an objection to some teleological argument. It states that there is a special fact about the world which is incompatible with the supposition that the world has been created by a good and omnipotent God. That special fact has something to do with the existence of evil in the world. The argument is thus a formulation of the celebrated "problem of evil."

Many of these formulations are rather weak, however. For example, hardly anyone doubts that there are evils in the world, and many people, including many theists, find it difficult to say just *why* they are there. That question is especially difficult if we demand specific reasons for particular evils: this war, that accident, and so forth. But the difficulty of this question or the inability of some theist to answer it does not of itself constitute a clear ground for denying that God exists. An antitheist who wants to develop this argument must find some positive way of drawing his conclusion—perhaps from some statement about evil and from some other premises.

Attempts to formulate this kind of argument are represented here by the selection from David Hume, whose treatment is one of the most famous and influential. Although parts of his presentation could be considered independent arguments against the existence of God, Hume himself thinks of his remarks primarily as demonstrating weaknesses in teleological type arguments. He says that independent knowledge of God's existence, if it were attainable, could easily be reconciled with the existence of evil. If, however, we are restricted to teleological type arguments for such knowledge, then the presence of evil in the world seriously weakens our arguments by suggesting that there is not as much order as we might expect if God existed or that it is not the kind of order we might expect. Some other versions of arguments from evil are cited in the bibliography, along with some of the better recent attempts to refute them.

A third line of antitheistic attack has gained philosophical prominence mainly in the last forty years, though it began to emerge much earlier. This is the claim that many characteristic assertions about God are not even false, but rather nonsensical; they have no cognitive status at all, not even that of falsehoods. This view originated from a special philosophical theory of language, called "logical positivism." Adherents of this theory attempted to restrict the cognitive and assertive use of language to statements which could be tested by sense perception. A number of very sophisticated attempts to formulate the positivist criterion for cognitive statements were shown to be failures, however. No one could formulate a criterion which was satisfied by ordinary scientific statements without being satisfied at the same time by all theological statements. For when the criteria were made strong enough to exclude some statements about God then a large body of ordinary and useful scientific statements were also ruled out as nonsensical! As a consequence of this failure, interest in the program of the logical positivists is now rather low. The application of their reasoning to statements about God is still popular among some philosophers, however, though it suffers seriously from the lack of a coherent formulation of its guiding principle. No examples of this sort of attack are presented below, but several relevant works are cited in the bibliography.

III. DIRECT EXPERIENCE

EXPERIENCE VS. ARGUMENT   A person's belief in the existence of something would probably appear rational if he had some direct experience of that thing; if, for example, the thing to be believed in were the Taj Mahal and the person had actually seen it. A person's belief in the existence of God would also appear rational if he had had some direct experience of God. In fact, many people from ancient times to the present have attested to such experiences, and some philosophers have attempted to assess the significance of this experience.

Much less work has been done on experiential theories than on proofs, however, and much it is fundamentally misdirected. There is probably one important reason for the inadequacy of this work. If a person's belief in God rests upon some argument, then he can express that argument to someone else in a book or lecture. The other person can then examine the evidence for his belief and evaluate it, criticize it, accept it, or reject it. For the argument consists only of a set of statements, and in reproducing that set in a book, a person reproduces all there is to the argument. But with a direct experience the situation is quite different. A person may visit the Taj Mahal, see it with his own eyes, run his hands over the masonry, and so forth. And he may write or lecture about it. But what he puts in his book is not his experience of the building, but merely *an account* of that experience. The description of an experience belongs to a radically different category from that of the experience itself.

This qualitative difference does not result from a faulty or incomplete description. For even if the person should report every detail of his experience we would still have only a report and not the experience itself. And it is not always true that we can learn more from experience than from reports. One person may be so much more careful an observer than another that the other could learn more from studying the report than he could from seeing the Taj Mahal himself. But even so, he would not have the same experience as the author of the report or even a similar one. He would have only a description.

Philosophers are notoriously denizens of the library and the lecture hall, and they are often uncomfortable with what cannot conveniently be captured there. Since the alleged experience of God cannot be produced as readily and reliably as a book or lecture it has been correspondingly shunned. (Chemistry lecturers, of course, sometimes provide relevant experience for their students in the lecture hall through demonstration experiments which supplement their descriptions. This experience is somewhat harder to provide in the case of, say, astronomy. And religious experience may be harder yet to provide.) Furthermore, when philosophers have dealt with this topic they have sometimes assumed that what can be put in books, that is, the description, is the basis of the belief. They have therefore treated the description as if it were the premise of an argument whose conclusion is some theological belief. And they have then proceeded to determine whether this argument is valid, and so forth. This assumption lies behind much of the procedure of C. B. Martin in the paper cited in the bibliography. But this approach involves a serious misconstruction of the situation. *The experience itself, and not its description, is the basis of the belief.* The relation of an experience to a belief cannot be like the relation of a premise to a conclusion, because an experience is not a statement.

For these reasons, we cannot expect philosophical considerations to be decisive in this area, or even as important as in a consideration of arguments. (But we must remember that philosophical considerations of arguments might not help us much in deciding about the truth of some premise either.) In any case, we should not expect religious questions to be fully decidable by any "armchair" methodology.

ONE PERSON'S EXPERIENCE AND ANOTHER'S The distinction

suggested in the preceding section is closely related to the distinction between a person's own experience and that of other people. One might, for example, approach the question of God's existence first by noting that many people have reported and described religious experiences and then by attempting to see whether these descriptions require the existence of God for their explanation. A person might do this even if he had no similar experience himself. In this case he would, of course, be working from the reports and descriptions of experience, and an analysis like the one appropriate for arguments might be in order. No approach of this kind is reprinted below, but the essay by C. D. Broad, cited in the bibliography, presents a balanced account of the more important considerations.

More interesting, however, is the suggestion by a number of writers that their belief rests upon *their own* experience of God; they assert that other people who are interested in this aspect of reality should not rely on the alleged experience of these authors but should watch for such experiences *in their own lives*. One such type of experience, the "mystical," is usually marked—whatever its theological significance may be—by unusual states of consciousness, trance, lack of awareness of events in the immediate environment, and so forth. No selections given below represent such experience, but there are references to this subject in the bibliography. Other writers have suggested, however, that much more common types of experience which either are experiences of God or would be such experiences if we interpreted them correctly. Among the selections reprinted below the one by John Baillie is the best example of this approach; probably the essay by C. S. Peirce also belongs in this category.

Peirce says explicitly that we have such experiences and that we could not have even the idea of God if we did not have them. But his later references to the role of instinct in this belief are puzzling. Perhaps his ideas could be restated as follows: "experience" means not merely bare sensations, whatever those might be, but something which includes interpretation or "the entire mental product." But the basic categories which we use in interpreting our experience—such as *physical object, person,* and so forth—as well as our choice of one category rather than another, are aspects of our mental life for which we can give no real reasons. For example, I am perfectly sure that the desk before me is a physical object and not a hallucination. But if I am asked just why I think so, then probably I will not be prepared to state a good reason for my belief. Any reasons which I might think up would probably be unconnected with that belief and would, in fact, be woefully weak when compared with its certainty. I suggest that this lack of ready reasons for the application of such fundamental categories is the real import of Peirce's references to *instinct*. He thinks also that when he interprets something as an experience of God he is, as in other cases, applying a fundamental category with certainty, although he can give no reason for it. And, of course, he goes on to claim that such rock-bottom, "instinctual" applications of categories to experience form the basis of all other intellectual operations, such as the formation of hypotheses, the construction of arguments, and so forth.

CRITICISM Most substantial criticisms of the experimental approach, for example that of Hepburn (see bibliography), focus on this lack of reasons. They point out that discussions of this type contain no clear criteria for distinguishing veridical from delusive religious experience. This may not be quite true, inasmuch as some mystics have attempted to give such rules of thumb, and a person who thinks he has had such an experience can always "compare notes" with other people as a check. But it is probably true that none of these suggested procedures is decisive and that the critic is largely correct on this point. The same objection can be made, however, in relation to any other kind of experience, ordinary sense experience for example. If this is so, then Peirce must have correctly described a fundamental feature of experience (whether we accept his "instinct" terminology or prefer some other) and the critic's search for a distinct criterion of veridicality is misdirected.

IV. CHOICE AS A BASIS OF RATIONALITY

THE VOLUNTARIST VIEW We shall now consider quite a different kind of answer to the question about the rationality of theistic belief. So far we have dealt with thinkers who tried to find reasons for such belief, or who at least claimed that they had reasons, and with their critics. (It is perhaps possible to interpret Peirce in such a way that he provides an exception to this description.) These thinkers and their critics would probably agree that a belief is rational if it is supported by a satisfactory reason. Some of them would hold the stronger view that a belief is rational *only if* it is supported by a satisfactory reason. But we shall now discuss thinkers who assert that some beliefs can be rational even though their truth is not supported by any reason.

A classical argument for this view is that of William James, reprinted below. (James' paper was perhaps provoked by W. K. Clifford's vigorous attack on this position, also reprinted below in part.) James himself qualifies his argument in various ways, and some of his examples may obscure rather than clarify its point. To understand his ideas better we might consider a somewhat stripped-down version of his type of argument: Accepting a belief, that is, believing something, is an act, and like other acts it has consequences—perhaps good, perhaps bad. The consequence which affects us is usually related to the truth or falsity of the belief. Usually the consequences are better if the belief is true than if it is false. The above statements about the relation of truth to consequences do not hold true for every case, however. For the moment we shall limit ourselves to those cases in which they do apply and return to the others later.

If we look at belief in this way we may think of it as analogous to a bet. In believing a statement we bet that it is true, and if it is true, we win—that is, we reap some good consequence. If it is false, of course, we lose. Evidence, reasons, and so forth constitute indications of whether the bet is more likely to win or to lose. (A conclusive reason would, of course, indicate a "sure thing.") This analysis of belief might appear to suggest that it is always better to believe in accordance with the evidence rather than against it, and that it would be futile to believe with no evidence at all, since such a belief could be false as easily as true. But this suggestion is in fact false, for the analysis so far has left out a crucial factor—what the gambler might call the "odds."

To see how important this factor can be let us suppose that a person is to roll a single die. Another person may bet either for or against the six turning up, and the payoff odds are ten to one (*e.g.*, if the six turns up the loser pays the winner ten dollars; if any other number comes up the loser pays the winner one dollar). Which is the preferable bet, the one to be chosen "rationally"? Of course, the six is unlikely to come up, so one who bets against it is likely to win something. But since the payoff odds favor the other bet it seems preferable. Though the person betting on the six is less likely to win, the amount to be won is so much larger that it more than compensates for the decreased probability. In a long series of such bets, the person who bets on the six will probably win an average of about eighty cents on each bet, and the person who bets against the six will lose at about that rate. The rule "Always bet on the most likely outcome" is therefore a very poor one for a better to follow, since it ignores the crucial factor of the payoffs. If believing is a kind of betting, or if believing is in any way an act performed for the sake of its consequences, then it seems reasonable to consider the payoffs along with the probabilities.

We can apply this factor to a special case, one in which we have no reason at all either for or against a certain proposed belief. This is probably what James means by an "intellectually unde-cidable" belief, and he includes belief in God's existence in this category. He also thinks that if a person believes in God and is right he will reap very valuable consequences, but if he believes in God and is mistaken his losses will be small. If James is right about these "payoffs" then the former belief certainly would be the preferable bet.

We need not, however, limit this kind of consideration to the special case in which we have no evidence either way. For as we saw earlier, a certain bet may be preferable even if the probabilities are against its success. If James is right about the consequences of theistic belief, then such a belief would be preferable even if there were some evidence against it. Furthermore, there seems to be no reason for restricting these considerations to cases which are "forced" or "momentous" as James does. This type of argument can be applied beyond the limits which James assigns to his own version.

In addition, some beliefs have consequences which are not related to their truth or falsity. Some, for example, may give us an esthetic satisfaction even if they happen to be false. But if, the beneficial consequences of a certain belief are great and the losses resulting from its falsity are small, then it might be rational to adopt this belief even if the evidence against it is conclusive! (In ordinary cases of betting it may sometimes be preferable to bet against a sure thing, since ordinary bets, too, can have consequences other than winning or losing.) This idea will, of course, strike some of us as very strange. But we probably cannot eliminate this surprising consequence in any consistent way without a thorough revision of this entire approach.

The selection from Soren Kierkegaard belongs in this category, since he defends the appropriateness (and the virtue) of passionate belief in the face of "objective uncertainty." In fact, he suggests, as James does not, that the virtue of religious belief would be weakened or perhaps destroyed entirely if there were any evidence in its favor. It is not certain that he would welcome a defense of his view like the one which I have sketched in the preceding paragraphs or the suggestion that he supports the "rationality" of ungrounded belief. This reluctance might result in part from his distaste for a terminology involving "reason" and its cognates. But perhaps it also has some deeper root. The reader should perhaps ask himself if he can formulate a defense of the views which Kierkegaard espouses.

CRITICISMS A number of criticisms have been made of the voluntarist view. Some critics have said, for example, that the proposal is impractical, since a person cannot believe simply by deciding to do so. And some have also claimed that James is mistaken in his estimate of the possible consequences of theistic belief.

These are no doubt important points. But perhaps the most interesting and far-reaching criticism arises if we pass over them for the moment. A view like that of James appears most plausible when put forth, as his is put forth, in a highly restricted form. If, however, the considerations which support the restricted version also support a much broader one we may profitably give some thought to the broader version; if it is unpalatable, there may be something fundamentally wrong with the supporting considerations.

If the more striking conclusions of the argument sketched earlier are disturbing, I suggest that the weakest link in this and similar arguments is the assumption that believing is an act performed for the sake of its consequences. If this assumption is false, then probably my version of the argument collapses. And I suspect that James' version depends upon such an assumption also.

V. ALTERNATIVE EXPLANATIONS OF BELIEF

PSYCHOLOGICAL ACCOUNTS Some people who assert that theistic belief is not rational have attempted to support this claim not merely by demolishing its professed rational bases (if, indeed, they do this at all), but also by providing alternative explanations of why that belief was adopted and continues to be held. These explanations are intended to show that the sources of such a belief are inadequate as grounds for its rationality. The most popular of such explanations at present are those which refer primarily to psychological factors. In one prominent approach of this type, theistic belief is viewed as a psychological mechanism defending someone against insufferable fear, insecurity, and so forth. The best representative of this approach is Sigmund Freud (see bibliography). He thinks that belief in God is an illusion generated by the desire for a universe as safe and comfortable as our childhood home with its strong and protective father. The existence of a cosmic father is projected, a magnified copy of a child's perception of his earthly father—powerful, wise, loving, and so forth. But, according to Freud, there is nothing in reality which gives any rational ground for believing that such a father exists. The real foundation of the belief is nothing but this childlike wish for security.

Now, it certainly seems that *if such an explanation of why people believe in God is true* then their belief is probably not rational. And there may be some evidence that something like this is the true explanation of why *certain people* hold theistic views. Unfortunately, however, psychological considerations often lead us one way as plausibly as another. It is not hard to see how a psychoanalytic explanation of atheism might account for atheistic views as displacements of, or disguises for, the individual's need to break away from his natural father, to reject him, or even to kill him. (Various pieces of "evidence" might be cited in favor of this view; *e.g.*, that many people begin to espouse atheistic views during adolescence, when conflicts with their natural parents are most acute.) We might also expect that a person who adopts atheistic views will rationalize them by arguing that theism is irrational. This point of view would provide, for what it was worth, a psychoanalytic account of Freud's own views and programs.

At this point we might take a more moderate position. Different people could possibly hold the same belief in very different ways. Some paranoid people, for example, believe quite irrationally that they are the objects of a murderous conspiracy. But some non-paranoid people are in fact the objects of a conspiracy, and they may have good reason to think so. Some people have hallucinations of snakes, but this does not prevent other people from actually seeing snakes and making a lifelong study of them, and so forth. Some people may therefore hold theistic beliefs irrationally, and similarly some atheists' beliefs may be caused in the manner described above. But it does not follow that all theists or atheists—or even most of them—are of this kind, or that a particular person's views are caused in this way. The reader attracted by Freud's account must ask himself whether there is any evidence that this account is true not merely of some pathological cases but of people in general.

RELIGIOUS BELIEF AS SELF-KNOWLEDGE   A somewhat different, and perhaps more profound, version of a psychological account is that of Ludwig Feuerbach, reprinted below. He thinks that religious belief is an attempt at self-knowledge—an attempt to know and grasp the essential elements of human nature by externalizing it, or, in other words, by imagining the external existence of a being who embodies an idealized version of our nature. God for Feuerbach is an imaginary being who embodies as perfectly as possible those human properties which we consider the "highest" and which distinguish us most sharply from the non-human world.

Feuerbach presents his view with a certain attractiveness and plausibility. But others have found equally plausible the view that man's "higher" properties and interests—his reason, intellect, and moral commitments, for example—are incomprehensible unless a

God actually exists embodying these properties to a superlative degree, from whom the human versions of these properties and commitments are derivative (*cf.* Thomas, Taylor, C. S. Lewis, Kant, Baillie, *etc.*). At first this conviction seems diametrically opposed to Feuerbach's. But perhaps they are not so far apart after all. For if the theists are right, it probably follows that profound self-knowledge cannot be attained—human nature cannot be understood in a coherent and satisfying way—unless the existence of such a being is envisaged. In a sense Feuerbach is also fundamentally right. The postulation of such a being is an essay in self-knowledge. But if the correctness of Feuerbach's positive thesis follows from the correctness of the theist's views, then Feuerbach's thesis does not refute these views. Or, to put it another way, we might accept Feuerbach's positive view—that the postulation of God's existence is an aid to self-knowledge—without committing ourselves to his negative view—that God is *only* an imaginary being. But again the reader attempting to decide this question must rely on his own experience and reflection.

VI. CONCLUSION

This essay has been intended merely as an introduction (perhaps in some cases a provocative introduction) to the selections which follow. A formal conclusion is therefore probably not necessary. Let me simply invite the reader who finds himself drawn toward the type of question which has been opened here to begin his own pilgrimage in good faith and with a ready mind.

Is the Nonexistence of God Conceivable?

St. Anselm (1033–1109) was a Benedictine monk whose philosophical views were deeply influenced by Plato. His major works are *Monologium, Proslogium,* and *Cur Deus Homo.* Gaunilon was an otherwise obscure contemporary of St. Anselm.

CHAPTER II

Truly there is a God, although the fool hath said in his heart, There is no God.

And so, Lord, do thou, who dost give understanding to faith, give me, so far as thou knowest it to be profitable, to understand that thou art as we believe; and that thou art that which we believe. And, indeed, we believe that thou art a being than which nothing greater can be conceived. Or is there no such nature, since the fool hath said in his heart, there is no God? (*Psalms* xiv. 1). But, at any rate, this very fool, when he hears of this being of which I speak—a being than which nothing greater can be conceived—understands

---

* From St. Anselm, *Proglogium* and *Apologetic,* and Gaunilon, *In Behalf of the Fool.* Reprinted from *St. Anselm: Basic Writings* with the permission of The Open Court Publishing Company, La Salle, Illinois.

what he hears, and what he understands is in his understanding; although he does not understand it to exist.

For, it is one thing for an object to be in the understanding, and another to understand that the object exists. When a painter first conceives of what he will afterwards perform, he has it in his understanding, but he does not yet understand it to be, because he has not yet performed it. But after he has made the painting, he both has it in his understanding, and he understands that it exists, because he has made it.

Hence, even the fool is convinced that something exists in the understanding, at least, than which nothing greater can be conceived. For, when he hears of this, he understands it. And whatever is understood, exists in the understanding. And assuredly that, than which nothing greater can be conceived, cannot exist in the understanding alone. For, suppose it exists in the understanding alone: then it can be conceived to exist in reality; which is greater.

Therefore, if that, than which nothing greater can be conceived, exists in the understanding alone, the very being, than which nothing greater can be conceived, is one, than which a greater can be conceived. But obviously this is impossible. Hence, there is no doubt that there exists a being, than which nothing greater can be conceived, and it exists both in the understanding and in reality.

CHAPTER III

God cannot be conceived not to exist.—God is that, than which nothing greater can be conceived.—That which can be conceived not to exist is not God.

And it assuredly exists so truly, that it cannot be conceived not to exist. For, it is possible to conceive of a being which cannot be conceived not to exist; and this is greater than one which can be conceived not to exist. Hence, if that, than which nothing greater can be conceived, can be conceived not to exist, it is not that, than which nothing greater can be conceived. But this is an irreconcilable contradiction. There is, then, so truly a being than which nothing greater can be conceived to exist, that it cannot even be conceived not to exist; and this being thou art, O Lord, our God.

So truly, therefore, dost thou exist, O Lord, my God, that thou canst not be conceived not to exist; and rightly. For, if a mind could conceive of a being better than thee, the creature would rise above the Creator; and this is most absurd. And, indeed, whatever else there is, except thee alone, can be conceived not to exist. To thee alone, therefore, it belongs to exist more truly than all other beings, and hence in a higher degree than all others. For, whatever else exists does not exist so truly, and hence in a less degree it belongs to it to exist. Why, then, has the fool said in his heart, there is no God (*Psalms* xiv. 1), since it is so evident, to a rational mind, that thou dost exist in the highest degree of all? Why, except that he is dull and a fool?

CHAPTER IV

How the fool has said in his heart what cannot be conceived.—A thing may be conceived in two ways: (1) when the word signifying it is conceived; (2) when the thing itself is understood. As far as the word goes, God can be conceived not to exist; in reality he cannot.

But how has the fool said in his heart what he could not conceive; or how is it that he could not conceive what he said in his heart, since it is the same to say in the heart, and to conceive?

But, if really, nay, since really, he both conceived, because he said in his heart; and did not say in his heart, because he could not conceive; there is more than one way in which a thing is said in the heart or conceived. For, in one sense, an object is conceived, when the word signifying it is conceived; and in another, when the very entity, which the object is, is understood.

In the former sense, then, God can be conceived not to exist; but in the latter, not at all. For no one who understands what fire and water are can conceive fire to be water, in accordance with the nature of the facts themselves, although this is possible according to the words. So, then, no one who understands what God is can conceive that God does not exist; although he says these words in his heart, either without any, or with some foreign, signification. For, God is that than which a greater cannot be conceived. And he who thoroughly understands this, assuredly understands that this being so truly exists, that not even in concept can it be nonexistent. Therefore, he who understands that God so exists, cannot conceive that he does not exist.

I thank thee, gracious Lord, I thank thee; because what I formerly believed by thy bounty, I now so understand by thine illumination, that if I were unwilling to believe that thou dost exist, I should not be able not to understand this to be true.

. . . .

IN BEHALF OF THE FOOL

An Answer to the argument of Anselm in the Proslogium, by Gaunilon, a monk of Marmoutier

(1) If one doubts or denies the existence of a being of such a nature that nothing greater than it can be conceived, he receives this answer:

The existence of this being is proved, in the first place, by the fact that he himself, in his doubt or denial regarding this being, already has it in his understanding; for in hearing it spoken of he understands what is spoken of. It is proved, therefore, by the fact that what he understands must exist not only in his understanding, but in reality also.

And the proof of this is as follows: It is a greater thing to exist both in the understanding and in reality than to be in the understanding alone. And if this being is in the understanding alone, whatever has even in the past existed in reality will be greater than this being. And so that which was greater than all beings will be less than some being, and will not be greater than all: which is a manifest contradiction.

And hence, that which is greater than all, already proved to be in the understanding, must exist not only in the understanding, but also in reality: for otherwise it will not be greater than all other beings.

(2) The fool might make this reply:

This being is said to be in my understanding already, only because I understand what is said. Now could it not with equal justice be said that I have in my understanding all manner of unreal objects, having absolutely no existence in themselves, because I understand these things if one speaks of them, whatever they may be?

Unless indeed it is shown that this being is of such a character that it cannot be held in concept like all unreal objects, or objects whose existence is uncertain: and hence I am not able to conceive of it when I hear of it, or to hold it in concept; but I must understand it and have it in my understanding; because, it seems, I cannot conceive of it in any other way than by understanding it, that is, by comprehending in my knowledge its existence in reality.

But if this is the case, in the first place there will be no distinction between what has precedence in time—namely, the having of an object in the understanding—and what is subsequent in time—namely, the understanding that an object exists; as in the example of the picture, which exists first in the mind of the painter, and afterwards in his work.

Moreover, the following assertion can hardly be accepted: that this being, when it is spoken of and heard of, cannot be conceived not to exist in the way in which even God can be conceived not to exist. For if this is impossible, what was the object of this argument against one who doubts or denies the existence of such a being?

Finally, that this being so exists that it cannot be perceived by an understanding convinced of its own indubitable existence, unless this being is afterwards conceived of—this should be proved to me by an indisputable argument, but not by that which you have advanced: namely, that what I understand, when I hear it, already is in my understanding. For thus in my understanding, as I still think, could be all sorts of things whose existence is uncertain, or which do not exist at all, if some one whose words I should understand mentioned them. And so much the more if I should be deceived, as often happens, and believe in them: though I do not yet believe in the being whose existence you would prove.

(3) Hence, your example of the painter who already has in his

understanding what he is to paint cannot agree with this argument. For the picture, before it is made, is contained in the artificer's art itself; and any such thing, existing in the art of an artificer, is nothing but a part of his understanding itself. A joiner, St. Augustine says, when he is about to make a box in fact, first has it in his art. The box which is made in fact is not life; but the box which exists in his art is life. For the artificer's soul lives, in which all these things are, before they are produced. Why, then, are these things life in the living soul of the artificer, unless because they are nothing else than the knowledge or understanding of the soul itself?

With the exception, however, of those facts which are known to pertain to the mental nature, whatever, on being heard and thought out by the understanding, is perceived to be real, undoubtedly that real object is one thing, and the understanding itself, by which the object is grasped, is another. Hence, even if it were true that there is a being than which a greater is inconceivable: yet to this being, when heard of and understood, the not yet created picture in the mind of the painter is not analogous.

(4) Let us notice also the point touched on above, with regard to this being which is greater than all which can be conceived, and which, it is said, can be none other than God himself. I, so far as actual knowledge of the object, either from its specific or general character, is concerned, am as little able to conceive of this being when I hear of it, or to have it in my understanding, as I am to conceive of or understand God himself: whom, indeed, for this very reason I can conceive not to exist. For I do not know that reality itself which God is, nor can I form a conjecture of that reality from some other like reality. For you yourself assert that that reality is such that there can be nothing else like it.

For, suppose that I should hear something said of a man absolutely unknown to me, of whose very existence I was unaware. Through that special or general knowledge by which I know what man is, or what men are, I could conceive of him also, according to the reality itself, which man is. And yet it would be possible, if the person who told me of him deceived me, that the man himself, of whom I conceived, did not exist; since that reality according to which I conceived of him, though a no less indisputable fact, was not that man, but any man.

Hence, I am not able, in the way in which I should have this unreal being in concept or in understanding, to have that being of which you speak in concept or in understanding, when I hear the word *God* or the words, *a being greater than all other beings.* For I can conceive of the man according to a fact that is real and familiar to me: but of God, or a being greater than all others, I could not conceive at all, except merely according to the word. And an object can hardly or never be conceived according to the word alone.

For when it is so conceived, it is not so much the word itself (which is, indeed, a real thing—that is, the sound of the letters and syllables) as the signification of the word, when heard, that is conceived. But it is not conceived as by one who knows what is generally signified by the word; by whom, that is, it is conceived according to a reality and in true conception alone. It is conceived as by a man who does not know the object, and conceives of it only in accordance with the movement of his mind produced by hearing the word, the mind attempting to image for itself the signification of the word that is heard. And it would be surprising if in the reality of fact it could ever attain to this.

Thus, it appears, and in no other way, this being is also in my understanding, when I hear and understand a person who says that there is a being greater than all conceivable beings. So much for the assertion that this supreme nature already is in my understanding.

(5) But that this being must exist, not only in the understanding but also in reality, is thus proved to me:

If it did not so exist, whatever exists in reality would be greater than it. And so the being which has been already proved to exist in my understanding, will not be greater than all other beings.

I still answer: if it should be said that a being which cannot be even conceived in terms of any fact, is in the understanding, I do not deny that this being is, accordingly, in my understanding. But since through this fact it can in no wise attain to real existence also, I do not yet concede to it that existence at all, until some certain proof of it shall be given.

For he who says that this being exists, because otherwise the being which is greater than all will not be greater than all, does not attend strictly enough to what he is saying. For I do not yet say, no, I even deny or doubt that this being is greater than any real object. Nor do I concede to it any other existence than this (if it should be called existence) which it has when the mind, according to a word merely heard, tries to form the image of an object absolutely unknown to it.

How, then, is the veritable existence of that being proved to me from the assumption, by hypothesis, that it is greater than all other beings? For I should still deny this, or doubt your demonstration of it, to this extent, that I should not admit that this being is in my understanding and concept even in the way in which many objects whose real existence is uncertain and doubtful, are in my understanding and concept. For it should be proved first that this being itself really exists somewhere; and then, from the fact that it is greater than all, we shall not hesitate to infer that it also subsists in itself.

(6) For example: it is said that somewhere in the ocean is an island, which, because of the difficulty, or rather the impossibility, of discovering what does not exist, is called the lost island. And they say that this island has an inestimable wealth of all manner of riches and delicacies in greater abundance than is told of the Islands of the Blest; and that having no owner or inhabitant, it is more excellent than all other countries, which are inhabited by mankind, in the abundance with which it is stored.

Now if some one should tell me that there is such an island, I should easily understand his words, in which there is no difficulty. But suppose that he went on to say, as if by a logical inference: "You can no longer doubt that this island which is more excellent than all lands exists somewhere, since you have no doubt that it is in your understanding. And since it is more excellent not to be in the understanding alone, but to exist both in the understanding and in reality, for this reason it must exist. For if it does not exist, any land which really exists will be more excellent than it; and so the island already understood by you to be more excellent will not be more excellent."

If a man should try to prove to me by such reasoning that this island truly exists, and that its existence should no longer be doubted, either I should believe that he was jesting, or I know not which I ought to regard as the greater fool: myself, supposing that I should allow this proof; or him, if he should suppose that he had established with any certainty the existence of this island. For he ought to show first that the hypothetical excellence of this island exists as a real and indubitable fact, and in no wise as any unreal object, or one whose existence is uncertain, in my understanding.

(7) This, in the mean time, is the answer the fool could make to the arguments urged against him. When he is assured in the first place that this being is so great that its nonexistence is not even conceivable, and that this in turn is proved on no other ground than the fact that otherwise it will not be greater than all things, the fool may make the same answer, and say:

When did I say that any such being exists in reality, that is, a being greater than all others? that on this ground it should be proved to me that it also exists in reality to such a degree that it cannot even be conceived not to exist? Whereas in the first place it should be in some way proved that a nature which is higher, that is, greater and better, than all other natures, exists; in order that from this we may then be able to prove all attributes which necessarily the being that is greater and better than all possesses.

Moreover, it is said that the nonexistence of this being is inconceivable. It might better be said, perhaps, that its nonexistence, or the possibility of its nonexistence, is unintelligible. For according to the true meaning of the word, unreal objects are unintelligible. Yet their existence is conceivable in the way in which the fool conceived of the nonexistence of God. I am most certainly aware of my own existence; but I know, nevertheless, that my nonexistence is possible. As to that supreme being, moreover, which God is, I understand without any doubt both his existence, and the impossibility of his nonexistence. Whether, however, so long as I am most positively aware of my existence, I can conceive of my nonexistence, I am not sure. But if I can, why can I not conceive of the nonexistence of whatever else I know with the same certainty? If, however, I cannot, God will not be the only being of which it can be said, it is impossible to conceive of his nonexistence.

(8) The other parts of this book are argued with such truth, such brilliancy, such grandeur; and are so replete with usefulness, so fragrant with a certain perfume of devout and holy feeling, that though there are matters in the beginning which, however rightly sensed, are weakly presented, the rest of the work should not be rejected on this account. The rather ought these earlier matters to be reasoned more cogently, and the whole to be received with great respect and honor.

[The following is part of Anselm's reply to Gaunilon.]

It was a fool against whom the argument of my Proslogium was directed. Seeing, however, that the author of these objections is by no means a fool, and is a Catholic, speaking in behalf of the fool, I think it sufficient that I answer the Catholic.

CHAPTER I

A general refutation of Gaunilon's argument. It is shown that a being than which a greater cannot be conceived exists in reality.

You say—whosoever you may be, who say that a fool is capable of making these statements—that a being than which a greater cannot be conceived is not in the understanding in any other sense than that in which a being that is altogether inconceivable in terms of reality, is in the understanding. You say that the inference that this being exists in reality, from the fact that it is in the understanding, is no more just than the inference that a lost island most certainly exists, from the fact that when it is described the hearer does not doubt that it is in his understanding.

But I say: if a being than which a greater is inconceivable is not understood or conceived, and is not in the understanding or in concept, certainly either God is not a being than which a greater is inconceivable, or else he is not understood or conceived, and is not in the understanding or in concept. But I call on your faith and conscience to attest that this is most false. Hence, that than which a greater cannot be conceived is truly understood and conceived, and is in the understanding and in concept. Therefore either the grounds on which you try to controvert me are not true, or else the inference which you think to base logically on those grounds is not justified.

But you hold, moreover, that supposing that a being than which a greater cannot be conceived is understood, it does not follow that this being is in the understanding; nor, if it is in the understanding, does it therefore exist in reality.

In answer to this, I maintain positively: if that being can be even conceived to be, it must exist in reality. For that than which a greater is inconceivable cannot be conceived except as without beginning. But whatever can be conceived to exist, and does not exist, can be conceived to exist through a beginning. Hence what can be conceived to exist, but does not exist, is not the being than which a greater cannot be conceived. Therefore, if such a being can be conceived to exist, necessarily it does exist.

Furthermore: if it can be conceived at all, it must exist. For no one who denies or doubts the existence of a being than which a greater is inconceivable, denies or doubts that if it did exist, its nonexistence, either in reality or in the understanding, would be impossible. For otherwise it would not be a being than which a greater cannot be conceived. But as to whatever can be conceived, but does not exist—if there were such a being, its nonexistence, either in reality or in the understanding, would be possible. Therefore if a being than which a greater is inconceivable can be even conceived, it cannot be nonexistent.

But let us suppose that it does not exist, even if it can be conceived. Whatever can be conceived, but does not exist, if it existed, would not be a being than which a greater is inconceivable. If, then, there were a being a greater than which is inconceivable, it would not be a being than which a greater is inconceivable: which is most absurd. Hence, it is false to deny that a being than which a greater cannot be conceived exists, if it can be even conceived;

much the more, therefore, if it can be understood or can be in the understanding.

Moreover, I will venture to make this assertion: without doubt, whatever at any place or at any time does not exist—even if it does exist at some place or at some time—can be conceived to exist nowhere and never, as at some place and at some time it does not exist. For what did not exist yesterday, and exists today, as it is understood not to have existed yesterday, so it can be apprehended by the intelligence that it never exists. And what is not here, and is elsewhere, can be conceived to be nowhere, just as it is not here. So with regard to an object of which the individual parts do not exist at the same places or times: all its parts and therefore its very whole can be conceived to exist nowhere or never.

For, although time is said to exist always, and the world everywhere, yet time does not as a whole exist always, nor the world as a whole everywhere. And as individual parts of time do not exist when others exist, so they can be conceived never to exist. And so it can be apprehended by the intelligence that individual parts of the world exist nowhere, as they do not exist where other parts exist. Moreover, what is composed of parts can be dissolved in concept, and be nonexistent. Therefore, whatever at any place or at any time does not exist as a whole, even if it is existent, can be conceived not to exist.

But that than which a greater cannot be conceived, if it exists, cannot be conceived not to exist. Otherwise, it is not a being than which a greater cannot be conceived: which is inconsistent. By no means, then, does it at any place or at any time fail to exist as a whole: but it exists as a whole everywhere and always.

Do you believe that this being can in some way be conceived or understood, or that the being with regard to which these things are understood can be in concept or in the understanding? For if it cannot, these things cannot be understood with reference to it. But if you say that it is not understood and that it is not in the understanding, because it is not thoroughly understood; you should say that a man who cannot face the direct rays of the sun does not see the light of day, which is none other than the sunlight. Assuredly a being than which a greater cannot be conceived exists, and is in the understanding, at least to this extent—that these statements regarding it are understood.

. . . .

CHAPTER V

A particular discussion of certain statements of Gaunilon's. In the first place, he misquoted the argument which he undertook to refute.

The nature of the other objections which you, in behalf of the fool, urge against me it is easy, even for a man of small wisdom, to detect; and I had therefore thought it unnecessary to show this. But since I hear that some readers of these objections think they have some weight against me, I will discuss them briefly.

In the first place, you often repeat that I assert that what is greater than all other beings is in the understanding; and if it is in the understanding, it exists also in reality, for otherwise the being which is greater than all would not be greater than all.

Nowhere in all my writings is such a demonstration found. For the real existence of a being which is said to be *greater than all other beings* cannot be demonstrated in the same way with the real existence of one that is said to be *a being than which a greater cannot be conceived.*

If it should be said that a being than which a greater cannot be conceived has no real existence, or that it is possible that it does not exist, or even that it can be conceived not to exist, such an assertion can be easily refuted. For the nonexistence of what does not exist is possible, and that whose nonexistence is possible can be conceived not to exist. But whatever can be conceived not to exist, if it exists, is not a being than which a greater cannot be conceived; but if it does not exist, it would not, even if it existed, be a being than which a greater cannot be conceived. But it cannot be said that a being than which a greater is inconceivable, if it exists, is not a being than which a greater is inconceivable; or that if it existed, it would not be a being than which a greater is inconceivable.

It is evident, then, that neither is it nonexistent, nor is it possible that it does not exist, nor can it be conceived not to exist. For otherwise, if it exists, it is not that which it is said to be in the hypothesis; and if it existed, it would not be what it is said to be in the hypothesis.

But this, it appears, cannot be so easily proved of a being which is said to be *greater than all other beings.* For it is not so evident that what can be conceived not to exist is not greater than all existing beings, as it is evident that it is not a being than which a greater cannot be conceived. Nor is it so indubitable that if a being greater than all other beings exists, it is no other than the being than which a greater cannot be conceived; or that if it were such a being, some other might not be this being in like manner; as it is certain with regard to a being which is hypothetically posited as one than which a greater cannot be conceived.

For consider: if one should say that there is a being greater than all other beings, and that this being can nevertheless be conceived not to exist; and that a being greater than this, although it does not exist, can be conceived to exist: can it be so clearly inferred in this case that this being is therefore not a being greater than all other existing beings, as it would be most positively affirmed in the other case, that the being under discussion is not, therefore, a being than which a greater cannot be conceived?

For the former conclusion requires another premise than the predication, *greater than all other beings.* In my argument, on the other hand, there is no need of any other than this very predication, *a being than which a greater cannot be conceived.*

If the same proof cannot be applied when the being in question is predicated to be greater than all others, which can be applied when it is predicated to be a being than which a greater cannot be conceived, you have unjustly censured me for saying what I did not say; since such a predication differs so greatly from that which I actually made. If, on the other hand, the other argument is valid, you ought not to blame me so for having said what can be proved.

Whether this can be proved, however, he will easily decide who recognises that this being than which a greater cannot be conceived is demonstrable. For by no means can this being than which a greater cannot be conceived be understood as any other than that which alone is greater than all. Hence, just as that than which a greater cannot be conceived is understood, and is in the understanding, and for that reason is asserted to exist in the reality of fact: so what is said to be greater than all other beings is understood and is in the understanding, and therefore it is necessarily inferred that it exists in reality.

You see, then, with how much justice you have compared me with your fool, who, on the sole ground that he understands what is described to him, would affirm that a lost island exists.

• • • • • • • • • • •

CHAPTER IX

The possibility of understanding and conceiving of the supremely great being. The argument advanced against the fool is confirmed.

But even if it were true that a being than which a greater is inconceivable cannot be conceived or understood; yet it would not be untrue that a being than which a greater cannot be conceived is conceivable and intelligible. There is nothing to prevent one's saying *ineffable,* although what is said to be ineffable cannot be spoken of. *Inconceivable* is conceivable, although that to which the word *inconceivable* can be applied is not conceivable. So, when one says, *that than which nothing greater is conceivable,* undoubtedly what is heard is conceivable and intelligible, although that being itself, than which a greater is inconceivable, cannot be conceived or understood.

Or, though there is a man so foolish as to say that there is no being than which a greater is inconceivable, he will not be so shameless as to say that he cannot understand or conceive of what he says. Or, if such a man is found, not only ought his words to be rejected, but he himself should be contemned.

Whoever, then, denies the existence of a being than which a greater cannot be conceived, at least understands and conceives of the denial which he makes. But this denial he cannot understand or conceive of without its component terms; and a term of this statement is *a being than which a greater cannot be conceived.* Whoever, then, makes this denial, understands and conceives of that than which a greater is inconceivable.

Moreover, it is evident that in the same way it is possible to conceive of and understand a being whose nonexistence is impossible; but he who conceives of this conceives of a greater being than one whose nonexistence is possible. Hence, when a being than which a greater is inconceivable is conceived, if it is a being whose nonexistence is possible that is conceived, it is not a being than which a greater cannot be conceived. But an object cannot be at once conceived and not conceived. Hence he who conceives of a being than which a greater is inconceivable, does not conceive of that whose nonexistence is possible, but of that whose nonexistence is impossible. Therefore, what he conceives of must exist; for anything whose nonexistence is possible, is not that of which he conceives.

. . . .

Five Proofs of God's Existence

Ways (handwritten above "Proofs")

St. Thomas Aquinas (1226–1274) was a member of the Dominican Order and a university lecturer. He wrote an enormous amount, his principal works being the *Summa Theologica* and the *Summa Contra Gentiles*.

WHETHER IT CAN BE DEMONSTRATED THAT GOD EXISTS?

We proceed thus to the Second Article:

Objection 1. It seems that the existence of God cannot be demonstrated. For it is an article of faith that God exists. But what is of faith cannot be demonstrated, because a demonstration produces scientific knowledge, whereas faith is of the unseen, as is clear from the Apostle (*Heb.* xi. 1). Therefore it cannot be demonstrated that God exists.

Objection 2. Further, essence is the middle term of demonstration. But we cannot know in what God's essence consists, but solely in what it does not consist, as Damascene says. Therefore we cannot demonstrate that God exists.

---

* From *Basic Writings of St. Thomas Aquinas*, Vol. I, edited by Anton C. Pegis. Copyright 1945 by Random House, Inc. Reprinted by permission of the publisher.

Objection 3. Further, if the existence of God were demonstrated, this could only be from His effects. But His effects are not proportioned to Him, since He is infinite and His effects are finite, and between the finite and infinite there is no proportion. Therefore, since a cause cannot be demonstrated by an effect not proportioned to it, it seems that the existence of God cannot be demonstrated.

On the contrary, The Apostle says: *The invisible things of Him are clearly seen, being understood by the things that are made* (*Rom.* i. 20). But this would not be unless the existence of God could be demonstrated through the things that are made; for the first thing we must know of anything is, whether it exists.

I answer that, Demonstration can be made in two ways: One is through the cause, and is called *propter quid,* and this is to argue from what is prior absolutely. The other is through the effect, and is called a demonstration *quia;* this is to argue from what is prior relatively only to us. When an effect is better known to us than its cause, from the effect we proceed to the knowledge of the cause. And from every effect the existence of its proper cause can be demonstrated, so long as its effects are better known to us; because, since every effect depends upon its cause, if the effect exists, the cause must preexist. Hence the existence of God, in so far as it is not self-evident to us, can be demonstrated from those of His effects which are known to us.

Reply Objection 1. The existence of God and other like truths about God, which can be known by natural reason, are not articles of faith, but are preambles to the articles; for faith presupposes natural knowledge, even as grace presupposes nature and perfection the perfectible. Nevertheless, there is nothing to prevent a man, who cannot grasp a proof, from accepting, as a matter of faith, something which in itself is capable of being scientifically known and demonstrated.

Reply Objection 2. When the existence of a cause is demonstrated from an effect, this effect takes the place of the definition of the cause in proving the cause's existence. This is especially the case in regard to God, because, in order to prove the existence of anything, it is necessary to accept as a middle term the meaning of the

name, and not its essence, for the question of its essence follows
on the question of its existence. Now the names given to God are
derived from His effects, as will be later shown. Consequently, in
demonstrating the existence of God from His effects, we may take
for the middle term the meaning of the name *God.*

Reply Objection 3. From effects not proportioned to the cause
no perfect knowledge of that cause can be obtained. Yet from every
effect the existence of the cause can be clearly demonstrated, and
so we can demonstrate the existence of God from His effects; though
from them we cannot know God perfectly as He is in His essence.

WHETHER GOD EXISTS?

We proceed thus to the Third Article:

Objection 1. It seems that God does not exist; because if one of
two contraries be infinite, the other would be altogether destroyed.
But the name *God* means that He is infinite goodness. If, therefore,
God existed, there would be no evil discoverable; but there is evil
in the world. Therefore God does not exist.

Objection 2. Further, it is superfluous to suppose that what can
be accounted for by a few principles has been produced by many.
But it seems that everything we see in the world can be accounted
for by other principles, supposing God did not exist. For all natural
things can be reduced to one principle, which is nature; and all
voluntary things can be reduced to one principle, which is human
reason, or will. Therefore there is no need to suppose God's existence.

On the contrary, It is said in the person of God: *I am Who am*
(*Exod.* iii. 14).

I answer that, The existence of God can be proved in five ways.

The first and more manifest way is the argument from motion.
It is certain, and evident to our senses, that in the world some
things are in motion. Now whatever is moved is moved by another,
for nothing can be moved except it is in potentiality to that
towards which it is moved; whereas a thing moves inasmuch as it
is in act. For motion is nothing else than the reduction of something from potentiality to actuality. But nothing can be reduced

from potentiality to actuality, except by something in a state of actuality. Thus that which is actually hot, as fire, makes wood, which is potentially hot, to be actually hot, and thereby moves and changes it. Now it is not possible that the same thing should be at once in actuality and potentiality in the same respect, but only in different respects. For what is actually hot cannot simultaneously be potentially hot; but it is simultaneously potentially cold. It is therefore impossible that in the same respect and in the same way a thing should be both mover and moved, that is, that it should move itself. Therefore, whatever is moved must be moved by another. If that by which it is moved be itself moved, then this also must needs be moved by another, and that by another again. But this cannot go on to infinity, because then there would be no first mover, and, consequently, no other mover, seeing that subsequent movers move only inasmuch as they are moved by the first mover; as the staff moves only because it is moved by the hand. Therefore it is necessary to arrive at a first mover, moved by no other; and this everyone understands to be God.

The second way is from the nature of efficient cause. In the world of sensible things we find there is an order of efficient causes. There is no case known (neither is it, indeed, possible) in which a thing is found to be the efficient cause of itself; for so it would be prior to itself, which is impossible. Now in efficient causes it is not possible to go on to infinity, because in all efficient causes following in order, the first is the cause of the intermediate cause, and the intermediate is the cause of the ultimate cause, whether the intermediate cause be several, or one only. Now to take away the cause is to take away the effect. Therefore, if there be no first cause among efficient causes, there will be no ultimate, nor any intermediate, cause. But if in efficient causes it is possible to go on to infinity, there will be no first efficient cause, neither will there be an ultimate effect, nor any intermediate efficient causes; all of which is plainly false. Therefore it is necessary to admit a first efficient cause, to which everyone gives the name of God.

The third way is taken from possibility and necessity, and runs thus. We find in nature things that are possible to be and not to be, since they are found to be generated, and to be corrupted, and consequently, it is possible for them to be and not to be. But it is impossible for these always to exist, for that which can not be at some time is not. Therefore, if everything can not be, then at one time there was nothing in existence. Now if this were true, even now there would be nothing in existence, because that which does not exist begins to exist only through something already existing. Therefore, if at one time nothing was in existence, it would have been impossible for anything to have begun to exist; and thus even now nothing would be in existence—which is absurd. Therefore, not all beings are merely possible, but there must exist something the existence of which is necessary. But every necessary thing either has its necessity caused by another, or not. Now it is impossible to go on to infinity in necessary things which have their necessity caused by another, as has been already proved in regard to efficient causes. Therefore we cannot but admit the existence of some being having of itself its own necessity, and not receiving it from another, but rather causing in others their necessity. This all men speak of as God.

The fourth way is taken from the gradation to be found in things. Among beings there are some more and some less good, true, noble, and the like. But *more* and *less* are predicated of different things according as they resemble in their different ways something which is the maximum, as a thing is said to be hotter according as it more nearly resembles that which is hottest; so that there is something which is truest, something best, something noblest, and, consequently, something which is most being, for those things that are greatest in truth are greatest in being, as it is written in *Metaphysics* ii. Now the maximum in any genus is the cause of all in that genus, as fire, which is the maximum of heat, is the cause of all hot things, as is said in the same book. Therefore there must also be something which is to all beings the cause of their being, goodness, and every other perfection; and this we call God.

The fifth way is taken from the governance of the world. We see that things which lack knowledge, such as natural bodies, act for an end, and this is evident from their acting always, or nearly always, in the same way, so as to obtain the best result. Hence it is plain that they achieve their end, not fortuitously, but designedly.

Now whatever lacks knowledge cannot move towards an end, unless it be directed by some being endowed with knowledge and intelligence; as the arrow is directed by the archer. Therefore some intelligent being exists by whom all natural things are directed to their end; and this being we call God.

Reply Objection 1. As Augustine says: *Since God is the highest good, He would not allow any evil to exist in His works, unless His omnipotence and goodness were such as to bring good even out of evil.* This is part of the infinite goodness of God, that He should allow evil to exist, and out of it produce good.

Reply Objection 2. Since nature works for a determinate end under the direction of a higher agent, whatever is done by nature must be traced back to God as to its first cause. So likewise whatever is done voluntarily must be traced back to some higher cause other than human reason and will, since these can change and fail; for all things that are changeable and capable of defect must be traced back to an immovable and self-necessary first principle, as has been shown.

Comments on
St. Thomas' Five Ways

~~~~~~

Frederick C. Copleston (1907–   ), a member of the Jesuit order, is a contemporary British philosopher and historian of philosophy. His major published work is *History of Philosophy* in several volumes.

•   •   •   •   •   •   •   •   •   •   •

Aquinas did not, of course, deny that people can come to know that God exists by other ways than by philosophic reflection. Nor did he ever assert that the belief of most people who accept the proposition that God exists is the result of their having elaborated metaphysical arguments for themselves or of their having thought through the metaphysical arguments developed by others. Nor did he confuse a purely intellectual assent to the conclusion of such a metaphysical argument with a living Christian faith in and love of God. But he did think that reflection on quite familiar features of the world affords ample evidence of God's existence. The reflection itself, sustained and developed at the metaphysical level, is difficult, and he explicitly recognized and acknowledged its dif-

* From F. C. Copleston, *Aquinas.* Reprinted with the permission of Penguin Books, publisher.

ficulty: he certainly did not consider that everyone is capable of sustained metaphysical reflection. At the same time the empirical facts on which this reflection is based were for him quite familiar facts. In order to see the relation of finite things to the being on which they depend we are not required to pursue scientific research, discovering hitherto unknown empirical facts. Nor does the metaphysician discover God in a manner analogous to the explorer who suddenly comes upon a hitherto unknown island or flower. It is attention and reflection which are required rather than research or exploration.

What, then, are the familiar facts which for Aquinas imply the existence of God? Mention of them can be found in the famous "five ways" of proving God's existence, which are outlined in the *Summa Theologica* (1a, 2, 3). In the first way Aquinas begins by saying that "it is certain, and it is clear from sense-experience, that some things in this world are moved." It must be remembered that he, like Aristotle, understands the term "motion" in the broad sense of change, reduction from a state of potentiality to one of act; he does not refer exclusively to local motion. In the second way he starts with the remark that "we find in material things an order of efficient causes." In other words, in our experience of things and of their relations to one another we are aware of efficient causality. Thus while in the first way he begins with the fact that some things are in motion or in a state of change, the second way is based upon the fact that some things act upon other things, as efficient causes. In the third way he starts by stating that "we find among things some which are capable of existing or not existing, since we find that some things come into being and pass away." In other words, we perceive that some things are corruptible or perishable. In the fourth proof he observes that "we find in things that some are more or less good and true and noble and so on (than others)." Finally in the fifth way he says: "we see that some things which lack knowledge, namely natural bodies, act for an end, which is clear from the fact that they always or in most cases act in the same way, in order to attain what is best."

There is, I think, little difficulty in accepting as empirical facts the starting points of the first three ways. For nobody really doubts that some things are acted upon and changed or "moved," that some things act on others, and that some things are perishable. Each of us is aware, for example, that he is acted upon and changed, that he sometimes acts as an efficient cause, and that he is perishable. Even if anyone were to cavil at the assertion that he is aware that he himself was born and will die, he knows very well that some other people were born and have died. But the starting points of the two final arguments may cause some difficulty. The proposition that there are different grades of perfections in things stands in need of a much more thorough analysis than Aquinas accords it in his brief outline of the fourth way. For the schematic outlining of the five proofs was designed, not to satisfy the critical minds of mature philosophers, but as introductory material for "novices" in the study of theology. And in any case Aquinas could naturally take for granted in the thirteenth century ideas which were familiar to his contemporaries and which had not yet been subjected to the radical criticism to which they were later subjected. At the same time there is not very much difficulty in understanding the sort of thing which was meant. We are all accustomed to think and speak as though, for example, there were different degrees of intelligence and intellectual capacity. In order to estimate the different degrees we need, it is true, standards or fixed points of reference; but, given these points of reference, we are all accustomed to make statements which imply different grades of perfections. And though these statements stand in need of close analysis, they refer to something which falls within ordinary experience and finds expression in ordinary language. As for the fifth way, the modern reader may find great difficulty in seeing what is meant if he confines his attention to the relevant passage in the *Summa Theologica*. But if he looks at the *Summa contra Gentiles* (1, 13) he will find Aquinas saying that we see things of different natures cooperating in the production and maintenance of a relatively stable order or system. When Aquinas says that we see purely material things acting for an end, he does not mean to say that they act in a manner analogous to that in which human beings consciously act for definite purposes. Indeed, the point of the argument is that they do not do so. He means that different kinds of things, like fire and water, the behaviour of which is determined by their several "forms," cooperate, not consciously but as a matter of fact, in such a way that there is a relatively stable order or system. And here again, though much more would need to be said in a full discussion of the matter, the basic idea is nothing particularly extraordinary nor is it contrary to our ordinary experience and expectations.

It is to be noted also that Aquinas speaks with considerable restraint: he avoids sweeping generalizations. Thus in the first argument he does not say that all material things are "moved" but that we see that some things in this world are moved or changed. In the third argument he does not state that all finite things are contingent but that we are aware that some things come into being and pass away. And in the fifth argument he does not say that there is an invariable world-order or system but that we see natural bodies acting always or in most cases in the same ways. The difficulty, therefore, which may be experienced in regard to Aquinas' proofs of God's existence concerns not so much the empirical facts or alleged empirical facts with which he starts as in seeing that these facts imply God's existence.

Perhaps a word should be said at once about this idea of "implication." As a matter of fact Aquinas does not use the word when talking about the five ways: he speaks of "proof" and of "demonstration." And by "demonstration" he means in this context what he calls *demonstratio quia* (S. T., 1a, 2, 2), namely a causal proof of God's existence, proceeding from the affirmation of some empirical fact, for example that there are things which change, to the affirmation of a transcendent cause. It is, indeed, his second proof which is strictly the causal argument, in the sense that it deals explicitly with the order of efficient causality; but in every proof the idea of ontological dependence on a transcendent cause appears in some form or other. Aquinas' conviction was that a full understanding of the empirical facts which are selected for consideration in the five ways involves seeing the dependence of these facts on a transcendent cause. The existence of things which change, for instance, is, in his opinion, not self-explanatory: it can be rendered intelligible only if seen as dependent on a transcendent cause, a cause, that is to say, which does not itself belong to the order of changing things.

This may suggest to the modern reader that Aquinas was concerned with causal explanation in the sense that he was concerned with framing an empirical hypothesis to explain certain facts. But he did not regard the proposition affirming God's existence as a causal hypothesis in the sense of being in principle revisable, as a hypothesis, that is to say, which might conceivably have to be revised in the light of fresh empirical data or which might be supplanted by a more economical hypothesis. This point can perhaps be seen most clearly in the case of his third argument, which is based on the fact that there are things which come into being and pass away. In Aquinas' opinion no fresh scientific knowledge about the physical constitution of such things could affect the validity of the argument. He did not look on a "demonstration" of God's existence as an empirical hypothesis in the sense in which the electronic theory, for example, is said to be an empirical hypothesis. It is, of course, open to anyone to say that in his own opinion cosmological arguments in favour of God's existence are in fact analogous to the empirical hypotheses of the sciences and that they have a predictive function; but it does not follow that this interpretation can legitimately be ascribed to Aquinas. We should not be misled by the illustrations which he sometimes offers from contemporary scientific theory. For these are mere illustrations to elucidate a point in terms easily understandable by his readers: they are not meant to indicate that the proofs of God's existence were for him empirical hypotheses in the modern sense of the term.

Does this mean, therefore, that Aquinas regarded the existence of God as being logically entailed by facts such as change or coming into being and passing away? He did not, of course, regard the proposition "there are things which come into being and pass away" as logically entailing the proposition "there is an absolutely necessary or independent being" in the sense that affirmation of the one proposition and denial of the other involves one in a verbal or formal linguistic contradiction. But he thought that metaphysical analysis of what it objectively means to be a thing which comes into being and passes away shows that such a thing must depend existentially on an absolutely necessary being. And he thought that metaphysical analysis of what it objectively means to be a changing thing shows that such a thing depends on a supreme unmoved mover. It follows that for Aquinas one is involved in a contradiction if one affirms the propositions "there are things which come into being and pass away" and "there are things which change" and at the same time denies the propositions "there is an absolutely necessary being" and "there is a supreme unmoved mover." But the contradiction can be made apparent only by means of metaphysical analysis. And the entailment in question is fundamentally an ontological or causal entailment.

Not a few philosophers (certainly all "empiricists") would presumably comment that if this represents Aquinas' real mind it is clear that he confused the causal relation with logical entailment. But it should be remembered that though Aquinas was convinced that the proposition stating that everything which begins to exist has a cause is absolutely certain he did not think that the existence of any finite thing entails the existence of any other finite thing in the sense that the existence of any finite thing can be said to entail the existence of God. In theological language, if we once admit that there is an omnipotent Creator, we can say that He could create and maintain in existence any finite thing without the existence of any other finite thing. But it does not follow that there can be any finite thing without God. In other words, Aquinas is not bound to produce other instances of the ontological entailment which he asserts between the existence of finite things and God. Though the relation of creatures to God is analogous in some way to the relation of causal dependence of one finite thing on another, the former relation is, if we consider it as such, unique. Aquinas was not confusing causal relations in general with logical entailments: he was asserting a unique relation between finite things and the transfinite transcendent cause on which they depend.

It is worth emphasizing perhaps that it does not necessarily follow from Aquinas' view that a metaphysical approach to God's existence is an easy matter. It is true that he was confident of the power of the human reason to attain knowledge of God's existence; and he did not regard his arguments as standing in need of support from rhetoric or emotional appeal. And in the *Summa Theologica*, where he is writing for "novices" in theology, he states the arguments in a bald and perhaps disconcertingly impersonal manner. But we cannot legitimately conclude that he thought it easy for a man to come to the knowledge of God's existence by philosophic reflection alone. Indeed, he makes an explicit statement to the opposite effect. He was well aware that in human life other factors besides metaphysical reflection exercise a great influence. Moreover, he would obviously agree that it is always possible to stop the process of reflection at a particular point. For Aquinas every being, in so far as it is or has being, is intelligible. But we can consider things from different points of view or under different aspects. For example, I might consider coming-into-being and passing-away simply in regard to definite instances and from a subjective point of view. It grieves me to think that someone I love will probably die before me and leave, as we say, a gap in my life. Or it grieves me to think that I shall die and be unable to complete the work which I have undertaken. Or I might consider coming-into-being and passing-away from some scientific point of view. What are the finite phenomenal causes of organic decay or of the generation of an organism? But I can also consider coming-into-being and passing-away purely as such and objectively, adopting a metaphysical point of view and directing my attention to the sort of being, considered as such, which is capable of coming into being and passing away. Nobody can compel me to adopt this point of view. If I am determined to remain on the level of, say, some particular science, I remain there; and that is that. Metaphysical reflections will have no meaning for me. But the metaphysical point of view is a possible point of view, and metaphysical reflection belongs to a full understanding of things so far as this is possible for a finite mind. And if I do adopt this point of view and maintain it in sustained reflection, an existential relation of dependence, Aquinas was convinced, should become clear to me which will not become clear to me if I remain on a different level of reflection. But just as extraneous factors (such as the influence of the general outlook promoted by a technical civilization) may help to produce my decision to remain on a nonmetaphysical level of reflection, so also can extraneous factors influence my reflections on the metaphysical level. It seems to me quite wrong to suggest that Aquinas did not regard metaphysical reflection as a possible way of becoming aware of God's existence and that he looked on it, as some writers have suggested, as being simply a rational justification of an assurance which is necessarily attained in some other way. For if it constitutes a rational justification at all, it must, I think, be a possible way of becoming aware of God's existence. But it does not necessarily follow, of course, that it is an easy way or a common way.

After these general remarks I turn to Aquinas' five proofs of the existence of God. In the first proof he argues that "motion" or change means the reduction of a thing from a state of potentiality to one of act, and that a thing cannot be reduced from potentiality to act except under the influence of an agent already in act. In this sense "everything which is moved must be moved by another." He argues finally that in order to avoid an infinite regress in the chain of movers, the existence of a first unmoved mover must be admitted. "And all understand that this is God."

A statement like "all understand that this is God" or "all call this (being) God" occurs at the end of each proof, and I postpone consideration of it for the moment. As for the ruling out of an infinite regress, I shall explain what Aquinas means to reject after outlining the second proof, which is similar in structure to the first.

Whereas in the first proof Aquinas considers things as being acted upon, as being changed or "moved," in the second he considers them as active agents, as efficient causes. He argues that there is a hierarchy of efficient causes, a subordinate cause being dependent on the cause above it in the hierarchy. He then proceeds, after excluding the hypothesis of an infinite regress, to draw the conclusion that there must be a first efficient cause, "which all call God."

Now, it is obviously impossible to discuss these arguments profitably unless they are first understood. And misunderstanding of them is only too easy, since the terms and phrases used are either unfamiliar or liable to be taken in a sense other than the sense intended. In the first place it is essential to understand that in the first argument Aquinas supposes that movement or change is dependent on a "mover" acting here and now, and that in the second argument he supposes that there are efficient causes in the world which even in their causal activity are here and now dependent on the causal activity of other causes. That is why I have spoken of a "hierarchy" rather than of a "series." What he is thinking of can be illustrated in this way. A son is dependent on his father, in the sense that he would not have existed except for the causal activity of his father. But when the son acts for himself, he is not dependent here and now on his father. But he is dependent here and now on other factors. Without the activity of the air, for instance, he could not himself act, and the life-preserving activity of the air is itself dependent here and now on other factors, and they in turn on other factors. I do not say that this illustration is in all respects adequate for the purpose; but it at least illustrates the fact that when Aquinas talks about an "order" of efficient causes he is not thinking of a series stretching back into the past, but of a hierarchy of causes, in which a subordinate member is here and now dependent on the causal activity of a higher member. If I wind up my watch at night, it then proceeds to work without further interference on my part. But the activity of the pen tracing these words on the page is here and now dependent on the activity of my hand, which in turn is here and now dependent on other factors.

The meaning of the rejection of an infinite regress should now be clear. Aquinas is not rejecting the possibility of an infinite series as such. We have already seen that he did not think that anyone had ever succeeded in showing the impossibility of an infinite series of events stretching back into the past. Therefore he does not mean to rule out the possibility of an infinite series of causes and effects, in which a given member depended on the preceding member, say X on Y, but does not, once it exists, depend here and now on the present causal activity of the preceding member. We have to imagine, not a lineal or horizontal series, so to speak, but a vertical hierarchy, in which a lower member depends here and now on the present causal activity of the member above it. It is the latter type of series, if prolonged to infinity, which Aquinas rejects. And he rejects it on the ground that unless there is a "first" member, a mover which is not itself moved or a cause which does not itself depend on the causal activity of a higher cause, it is not possible to explain the "motion" or the causal activity of the lowest member. His point of view is this. Suppress the first unmoved mover and there is no motion or change here and now. Suppress the first efficient cause and there is no causal activity here and now. If therefore we find that some things in the world are changed, there must be a first unmoved mover. And if there are efficient causes in the world, there must be a first efficient, and completely nondependent cause. The word "first" does not mean first in the temporal order, but supreme or first in the onto-logical order.

A remark on the word "cause" is here in place. What precisely Aquinas would have said to the David Humes either of the four-teenth century or of the modern era it is obviously impossible to say. But it is clear that he believed in real causal efficacy and real causal relations. He was aware, of course, that causal efficacy is not the object of vision in the sense in which patches of colours are objects of vision; but the human being, he considered, is aware of real causal relations and if we understand "perception" as in-volving the cooperation of sense and intellect, we can be said to "perceive" causality. And presumably he would have said that the sufficiency of a phenomenalistic interpretation of causality for purposes of physical science proves nothing against the validity of a metaphysical notion of causality. It is obviously possible to dis-pute whether his analyses of change or "motion" and of efficient causality are valid or invalid and whether there is such a thing as a hierarchy of causes. And our opinion about the validity or in-validity of his arguments for the existence of God will depend very largely on our answers to these questions. But mention of the mathematical infinite series is irrelevant to a discussion of his argu-ments. And it is this point which I have been trying to make clear.

In the third proof Aquinas starts from the fact that some things come into being and perish, and he concludes from this that it is possible for them to exist or not to exist: they do not exist "necessarily." He then argues that it is impossible for things which are of this kind to exist always; for "that which is capable of not existing, at some time does not exist." If all things were of this kind, at some time there would be nothing. Aquinas is clearly supposing for the sake of argument the hypothesis of infinite time, and his proof is designed to cover this hypothesis. He does not say that infinite time is impossible: what he says is that if time is infinite and if all things are capable of not existing, this potentiality would inevitably be fulfilled in infinite time. There would then be nothing. And if there had ever been nothing, nothing would now exist. For no thing can bring itself into existence. But it is clear as a matter of fact that there are things. Therefore it can never have been true to say that there was literally no thing. Therefore it is impossible that all things should be capable of existing or not existing. There must, then, be some necessary being. But perhaps it is necessary in the sense that it must exist if something else exists; that is to say, its necessity may be hypothetical. We cannot, however, proceed to infinity in the series or hierarchy of necessary beings. If we do so, we do not explain the presence here and now of beings capable of existing or not existing. Therefore we must affirm the existence of a being which is absolutely necessary (*per se necessarium*) and completely independent. "And all call this being *God.*"

This argument may appear to be quite unnecessarily complicated and obscure. But it has to be seen in its historical context. As already mentioned, Aquinas designed his argument in such a way as to be independent of the question whether or not the world existed from eternity. He wanted to show that on either hypothesis there must be a necessary being. As for the introduction of hypothetical necessary beings, he wanted to show that even if there are such beings, perhaps within the universe, which are not corruptible in the sense in which a flower is corruptible, there must still be an absolutely independent being. Finally, in regard to terminology, Aquinas uses the common medieval expression "necessary being." He does not actually use the term "contingent being" in the argument and talks instead about "possible" beings; but it comes to the same thing. And though the words "contingent" and "necessary" are now applied to propositions rather than to beings, I have retained Aquinas' mode of speaking. Whether one accepts the argument or not, I do not think that there is any insuperable difficulty in understanding the line of thought.

The fourth argument is admittedly difficult to grasp. Aquinas argues that there are degrees of perfections in things. Different kinds of finite things possess different perfections in diverse limited degrees. He then argues not only that if there are different degrees of a perfection like goodness there is a supreme good to which other good things approximate but also that all limited degrees of goodness are caused by the supreme good. And since goodness is a convertible term with being, a thing being good in so far as it has being, the supreme good is the supreme being and the cause of being in all other things. "Therefore there is something which is the cause of the being and goodness and of every perfection in all other things; and this we call *God.*"

Aquinas refers to some remarks of Aristotle in the *Metaphysics*; but this argument puts one in mind at once of Plato's *Symposium* and *Republic*. And the Platonic doctrine of participation seems to be involved. Aquinas was not immediately acquainted with either work, but the Platonic line of thought was familiar to him from other writers. And it has not disappeared from philosophy. Indeed, some of those theists who reject or doubt the validity of the "cosmological" arguments seem to feel a marked attraction for some variety of the fourth way, arguing that in the recognition of objective values we implicitly recognize God as the supreme value. But if the line of thought represented by the fourth way is to mean anything to the average modern reader, it has to be presented in a rather different manner from that in which it is expressed by Aquinas who was able to assume in his readers ideas and points of view which can no longer be presupposed.

Finally, the fifth proof, if we take its statement in the *Summa Theologica* together with that in the *Summa contra Gentiles*, can be expressed more or less as follows. The activity and behaviour of each thing is determined by its form. But we observe material things of very different types cooperating in such a way as to produce and maintain a relatively stable world-order or system. They achieve an "end," the production and maintenance of a cosmic order. But nonintelligent material things certainly do not cooperate consciously in view of a purpose. If it is said that they cooperate in the realization of an end or purpose, this does not mean that they intend the realization of this order in a manner analogous to that in which a man can act consciously with a view to the achievement of a purpose. Nor, when Aquinas talks about operating "for an end" in this connexion, is he thinking of the utility of certain things to the human race. He is not saying, for example, that grass grows to feed the sheep and that sheep exist in order that human beings should have food and clothing. It is of the unconscious cooperation of different kinds of material things in the production and maintenance of a relatively stable cosmic system that he is thinking, not of the benefits accruing to us from our use of certain objects. And his argument is that this cooperation on the part of heterogeneous material things clearly points to the existence of an extrinsic intelligent author of this cooperation, who operates with an end in view. If Aquinas had lived in the days of the evolutionary hypothesis, he would doubtless have argued that this hypothesis supports rather than invalidates the conclusion of the argument.

No one of these arguments was entirely new, as Aquinas himself was very well aware. But he developed them and arranged them to form a coherent whole. I do not mean that he regarded the validity of one particular argument as necessarily depending on the validity of the other four. He doubtless thought that each argument was valid in its own right. But, as I have already remarked, they conform to a certain pattern, and they are mutually complementary in the sense that in each argument things are considered from a different point of view or under a different aspect. They are so many different approaches to God.

ALFRED E. TAYLOR

Two Proofs of God's
Existence

Alfred E. Taylor (1869–1945) was a well-known Platonic scholar. He has written major works on Plato and Aristotle, as well as *The Faith of a Moralist, Does God Exist?*, and *The Christian Hope of Immortality.*

Speaking quite generally, I suppose we may say that no great and far-reaching scientific theory is ever adopted because it has been demonstrated. It is not believed because it can be shown by stringent logic that all other accounts of facts involve self-contradiction. The real reason for belief is that the theory provides a key for the interpretation of the facts on which it is said to be founded, that on further investigation it is found also to provide a key to the interpretation of numerous groups of often very dissimilar facts, which were either uninterpretable or actually unknown when the theory was first put forward, and that even where at first sight there are facts which seem refractory to the proposed interpretation, the general theory can be made to fit them by some modification which does not interfere with its continued use for the interpretation of the facts by which it was first suggested. In this respect the

* From A. E. Taylor, "The Vindication of Religion," in E. G. Selwyn, ed., *Essays Catholic and Critical.* Reprinted with the permission of The Society for Promoting Christian Knowledge and the Macmillan Co.

interpretation of the "book of Nature" is exactly similar to the process of deciphering a cryptogram or an inscription in a hitherto unknown language. The decipherer has first to be in possession of a "key" of promising make. Thus, the inscription may be bilingual and one language may be a known one; there may be good reasons for believing that the cipher message is in English, and this enables the reader to make a probable conjecture from the relative frequency of certain signs alone or in combination. The original identifications will usually be in part erroneous, but even where they are so, if enough of them are correct, the partial decipherment will make the words of the text sufficiently intelligible to lead to subsequent correction of initial mistakes; though, when all our ingenuity has been expended, it may still remain the case that some of the signs we are trying to decipher have to be left uninterpreted owing to the insufficiency of our data. If our inscription were interminable, we might readily have to acknowledge that, though successive scrutiny made each new reading more nearly correct than those which went before, a final and definitive transcription was beyond our reach, and that all we could do was to make the tenative and provisional element in our readings steadily smaller. It is hardly necessary to mention the way in which this tentative process of decipherment of symbols, applied to the hieroglyphs of Egypt and the cuneiform of Babylon, has already enriched our historical knowledge of the early civilisations by making real to us the politics and social life of people who, a few generations ago, were little but names to us, or the still greater flood of light on the past of our race which may yet come from the successful reading of Cretan and Hittite records.

•   •   •   •   •   ‾   •   •   ‾   ‾   •

If all this is so, we cannot be fairly asked to justify religion by producing a different kind of vindication, or a fuller degree of vindication, of the "religious view" of the world than the man of science would think adequate if he were called on to "vindicate" the "scientific view" of the world. In either case the most that can be demanded of us is to show that there are real and undeniable facts which call for explanation and must not be explained *away*; that the interpretation supplied brings coherence and "sense" into them, where they would, without it, be an unintelligible puzzle; that the more steadily and systematically the principles we fall back on are employed, the less puzzling does the reality we are trying to interpret become. In a word, we need to show that there is the same solid ground for holding that religion cannot be dismissed as a passing illusion incident to a particular stage in the mental growth of humanity as there is for holding the same view about science. If we cannot *demonstrate* that religion is not temporary illusion, neither can we *demonstrate* that science is in any better position. And it may be worth while to observe in express words that the real weight of the "evidence" which is accepted as sufficient ground for assurance can only be judged by a mind of the right kind and with the right training. This holds good without exception in all branches of "secular" learning. An experiment which the trained chemist or physicist sees to be "crucial" as deciding for or against a speculation will often seem of no particular significance to a layman; it requires another and a different type of mind and a different training to appreciate the sort of considerations which a trained palæographer will regard as decisive for the authenticity of a document, the soundness of a reading, the worth of a speculation about the relations between the various extant manuscripts of an ancient author.[1]

[1] This is why even men of high intellectual power so often make themselves merely ridiculous when they venture into fields of knowledge where they are amateurs. Their training has not prepared them to be sound judges of the kind of considerations which are decisive in dealing with the unfamiliar matter. It is notorious that some of the very worst Biblical and Shakespearian "criticism" has been produced by lawyers who are very sound judges of evidence within their own sphere. The trouble is that their training disposes them to assume that what cannot be "proved" under the rules of the English or some other law of evidence cannot be adequately established in history or in literary criticism, or that what would be regarded as sufficient evidence for a British jury must always be sufficient evidence for the historian or the critic. Both assumptions are mistaken. Thus a "lawyer turned apologist" will argue that the critical analysis of the Pentateuch must be rejected because no one can "produce to the court" copies of the earlier documents into which it is analysed, or again that he has proved the correctness of the traditional ascription of a work

. . . .

I. FROM NATURE TO GOD

(1) The argument "from Nature up to Nature's God" can be presented in very different forms and with very different degrees of persuasiveness, corresponding with the more or less definite and accurate knowledge of different ages about the detailed facts of Nature and the greater or less degree of articulation attained by Logic. But the main thought underlying these very different variations is throughout the same, that the incomplete points to the complete, the dependent to the independent, the temporal to the eternal. Nature, in the sense of the complex of "objects presented to our notice," the bodies animate and inanimate around us, and our own bodies which interact with them and each other, is, in the first place, always something incomplete; it has no limits or bounds; the horizon in space and time endlessly recedes as we carry our adventure of exploration further; "still beyond the sea, there is more sea." What is more, Nature is always dependent; no part of it contains its complete explanation in itself; to explain why any part is what it is, we have always to take into account the relations of that part with some other, which in turn requires for explanation its relation to a third, and so on without end. And the fuller and richer our knowledge of the content of Nature becomes, the more, not the less, imperative do we find the necessity of explaining everything by reference to other things which, in their turn, call for explanation in the same way. Again, mutability is stamped on the face of every part of Nature. "All things pass and nothing abides." What was here in the past is now here no more, and what is here now will some day no longer be here. "There stood the rock where rolls the sea." Even what looks at first like permanence turns out on closer examination to be only slower birth and decay. Even the Christian Middle Ages thought of the "heavens" as persisting unchanged from the day of their creation to that of their coming

---

like the Fourth Gospel to a particular author by merely showing that the tradition is ancient, as though some sort of law of "prescription" held good in questions of authorship.

dissolution in fiery heat and new creation; modern astronomy tells us of the gradual production and dissolution of whole "stellar systems." Thoughts like these suggested to the Greek mind from the very infancy of science the conclusion that Nature is no self-contained system which is its own *raison d'être.* Behind all temporality and change there must be something unchanging and eternal which is the source of all things mutable and the explanation why they are as they are. In the first instance this sense of mutability gave rise only to a desire to know what is the permanent stuff of which what we call "things" are only passing phases; is it water, or vapour, or fire, or perhaps something different from them all? The one question which was primary for the earliest men of science was just this question about the stuff of which everything is made. To us it seems a very different thing to say "all things are water," or to say "I believe in God," but at bottom the quest after the stuff of which things are made is a first uncertain and half-blind step in the same direction as Aristotle's famous argument, adopted by St. Thomas, for the existence of an "unmoved Mover" (who, remaining *immotus in se,* is the source of all the movement and life of this lower world), and as all the since familiar *a posteriori* proofs of the existence of God.

(2) It is but a further step in the same direction, which was soon taken by the early founders of science, when it is perceived that the persistence of an unchanged "stuff" is no complete explanation of the apparent facts of Nature, and that we have further to ask where the "motion" which is the life of all natural processes comes from. This is the form in which the problem presented itself to Aristotle and his great follower St. Thomas. They believed that "Nature is uniform" in the sense that all the apparently irregular and lawless movements and changes with which life makes us familiar in the world around us issue from, and are the effects of, other movements (those of the "heavens"), which are absolutely regular and uniform. On this view, the supreme dominant uniform movement in Nature is naturally identified with the apparently absolutely regular diurnal revolution of the whole stellar heavens round the earth. But Aristotle could not be content to accept the mere fact of this supposed revolution as an ultimate fact needing no further explana-

tion. No motion explains itself, and we have therefore to ask the "cause" or reason why the heavens should display this uniform continuous movement. That reason Aristotle and his followers could only explain in the language of imaginative myth. Since nothing can set itself going, the movement which pervades the whole universe of Nature must be set going by something which is not itself set going by anything else; not mutable and changeable therefore, but eternally selfsame and perfect, because it already is all that it can be, and so neither needs nor permits of development of any kind. "From such a principle depends the whole heaven." [2] And it follows from certain other presuppositions of Aristotle's philosophy that this "principle" must be thought of as a perfect and living intelligence. Thus in Aristotle's formulation of the principles of natural science we reach the explicit result that Nature is in its inmost structure only explicable as something which depends on a perfect and eternal source of life, and this source is not itself Nature nor any part of Nature; the "transcendence of God" has at last been explicitly affirmed as a truth suggested (Aristotle and St. Thomas would say demonstrated) by the rational analysis of Nature herself. In principle their argument is that of every later form of the "cosmological proof."

Meanwhile with the transference of interest from the question about the stuff of which things are made to the question of the source of their movement and life, another line of thought had become prominent. The connection between organ and function is one which naturally struck the faraway founders of the science of biology. For living things show adaptation to their environment, and the various organs of living beings show adaptation to the discharge of specific functions conducing to the maintenance of the individual or the kind. And again, the living creature is not equally adapted at all stages of its existence for the full discharge of these functions. We can see it adapting itself to one of the most important of these as we watch the series of changes it undergoes from infancy to puberty, and we see the same process more elaborately if we widen our horizon and study the prenatal

[2] Aristotle, *Metaphysics*, 1072*b*, 14.

history of the embryo. From such considerations derives the further suggestion which ultimately becomes the "argument from design." Aristotle is convinced that the biological analogy may be applied to all processes of the organic or inorganic world. Every process has a final stage or "end" in which it culminates, as the whole process of conception, birth, postnatal growth culminates in the existence of the physically adult animal; and it is always the "end" to which a process is relative that determines the character of the earlier stages of the process. One seed grows into an apple tree, another into a pear tree, not because the two have been differently pulled or pushed, heated or cooled, wetted or dried, but because from the first the one was the sort of thing which was going, if not interfered with, to become an apple, the other the sort of thing which was going to become a pear. In the same way, there is definite order or plan everywhere in the structure of Nature, though Aristotle, unlike his master Plato, will not account for this orderliness by appeal to the conscious will and beneficent intention of his supreme Intelligence, but regards it rather, in the fashion of many modern biologists, as due to an unconscious and instinctive "quasi-purposiveness" in Nature herself.[3]

Let us look back at this line of thought, out of which the familiar "proofs of the existence of God" brought forward in popular works on Natural Theology have been developed, and ask ourselves what permanent value it retains for us today and how far it goes towards suggesting the real existence of a God whom a religious man can worship "in spirit and in truth." We must not suppose that the thought itself is necessarily antiquated because the language in which it is clothed strikes us as old-fashioned, or because those who gave it its first expression held certain views about the details of Nature's structure (notably the geocentric conception in astronomy) which are now obsolete. It may very well be that the substitution of contemporary for anti-

[3] For an excellent summary account of the early Greek science referred to above see Burnet, *Greek Philosophy: Thales to Plato*, pp. 1–101; and for what has been said of Aristotle, W. D. Ross, *Aristotle*, Chap. iii, pp. 62–111, Chap. iv, pp. 112–128, and Chap. vi, pp. 179–186; or, for a briefer summary A. E. Taylor, *Aristotle* (Nelson & Sons, 1919), Chaps. iii–iv, pp. 49–98.

quated views about the structure of the "stellar universe" or the fixity of animal species will leave the force of the argument, whatever that force may be, unaffected. There are two criticisms in particular which it is as well to dispose of at once, since both sound plausible, and both, unless I am badly mistaken, go wide of the mark.

(a) The point of the argument about the necessity of an "unmoving source of motion" must not be missed. We shall grasp it better if we remember that "motion" in the vocabulary of Aristotle means change of every kind, so that what is being asserted is that there must be an unchanging cause or source of change. Also, we must not fancy that we have disposed of the argument by saying that there is no scientific presumption that the series of changes which make up the life of Nature may not have been without a beginning and destined to have no end. St. Thomas, whose famous five proofs of the existence of God are all of them variations on the argument from "motion," or, as we might say, the appeal to the principle of causality, was also the philosopher who created a sensation among the Christian thinkers of his day by insisting stiffly that, apart from the revelation given in Scripture, no reasons can be produced for holding that the world had a beginning or need have an end, as indeed Aristotle maintained that it has neither. The dependence meant in the argument has nothing to do with succession in time. What is really meant is that our knowledge of any event in Nature is not complete until we know the full reason for the event. So long as you only know that A is so because B is so, but cannot tell why B is so, your knowledge is incomplete. It only becomes complete when you are in a position to say that ultimately A is so because Z is so, Z being something which is its own *raison d'être*, and therefore such that it would be senseless to ask *why* Z is so. This at once leads to the conclusion that since we always have the right to ask about any event in Nature why that event is so, what are its conditions, the Z which is its own *raison d'être* cannot itself belong to Nature. The point of the reasoning is precisely that it is an argument from the fact that there is a "Nature" to the reality of a "Supernature," and this point is unaffected by the question whether there ever was a beginning of time, or a time when there were no "events."

Again, we must not be led off the track by the plausible but shallow remark that the whole problem about the "cause of motion" arose from the unnecessary assumption that things were once at rest and afterwards began to move, so that you have only to start, as the modern physicist does, with a plurality of moving particles, or atoms, or electrons to get rid of the whole question. Nor would it be relevant to remark that modern physics knows of no such absolutely uniform motions as those which Aristotle ascribes to "the heavens," but only of more or less stable motions. If you start, for example, with a system of "particles" all in uniform motion, you have still to account for the rise of "differential" motions. If you start, as Epicurus tried to do, with a rain of particles all moving in the same direction and with the same relative velocities, you cannot explain why these particles ever came together to form complexes. If you prefer, with Herbert Spencer, to start with a strictly "homogeneous" nebula, you have to explain, as Spencer does not, how "heterogeneity" ever got in. You must have individual variety, as well as "uniformity," in whatever you choose to take as your postulated original data if you are to get out of the data a world like ours, which, as Mill truly says, is not only uniform but also infinitely various. *Ex nihilo, nihil fit*, and equally out of blank uniformity nothing *fit* but a uniformity equally blank. Even if, *per impossibile*, you could exclude all individual variety from the initial data of a system of natural science, you might properly be asked to account for this singular absence of variety, and a naturalistic account of it could only take the form of deriving it from some more ultimate state of things which was not marked by absolute "uniformity." Neither uniformity nor variety is self-explanatory; whichever you start with, you are faced by the old dilemma. Either the initial data must simply be taken as brute "fact," for which there is no reason at all, or if there is a reason, it must be found outside Nature, in the "supernatural."

(b) Similarly, it does not dispose of the conception of natural processes as tending to an "end" and being at least "quasi-purposive" to say that the thought originated with men who knew nothing of "evolution" and falsely believed in the fixity of natural kinds. In point of fact the notion of the gradual development of existing natural species made its appearance at the very dawn of Greek science and was quite familiar to the great philosophers who gave the Greek tradition its definitive form, though they rejected it because, so far as they knew, the evidence of facts seemed against it. The admission of the reality of the "evolution" of fresh species has, however, no direct bearing on the question of "ends in Nature": it actually suggests the raising of that very question in a new form. Is there, or is there not, in organic evolution a general trend to the successive emergence of beings of increasing intelligence? And if so, must the process be supposed to have reached its culmination, so far as our planet is concerned, in man, or must man be regarded as a mere stage in the production of something better, a *Pfeil der Sehnsucht nach dem Uebermenschen*? These are questions which we are still asking ourselves today, and though the strict positivists among our scientific men may insist that they probably cannot be answered and that it is certainly not the business of natural science to answer them, it is at least curious that the scientific man not infrequently unconsciously betrays the fact that he has privately answered them to his own satisfaction by the very fact that he talks of "evolution" as "progress," a phrase which has no meaning except in relation to a goal or an end, or even, on occasion, permits himself to assume that what is "more fully evolved," that is, comes later in the course of a development, must obviously be brighter and better than whatever went before it. Thus the old problem is still with us and we cannot take it for granted that the old answers have lost their meaning or value.

We may, for example, consider how the old-fashioned argument from "motion" to the "unmoving" source of motion, when stated in its most general form, might still be urged even today. As we have seen, the argument is simply from the temporal, conditioned and mutable to something eternal, unconditioned and immutable as its source. The nerve of the whole reasoning is that every explanation of given facts or events involves bringing in reference to

further unexplained facts; a complete explanation of anything, if
we could obtain one, would therefore require that we should
trace the fact explained back to something which contains its own
explanation within itself, a something which is and is what it is
in its own right; such a something plainly is not an event or mere
fact and therefore not included in "Nature," the complex of all
events and facts, but "above" Nature. Any man has a right to
say, if he pleases, that he personally does not care to spend his
time in exercising this mode of thinking, but would rather occupy
himself in discovering fresh facts or fresh and hitherto unsuspected
relations between facts. We need not blame him for that; but we
are entitled to ask those who are alive to the meaning of the old
problem how they propose to deal with it, if they reject the
inference from the unfinished and conditioned to the perfect and
unconditioned. For my own part I can see only two alternatives.

(1) One is to say, as Hume[4] did in his "Dialogues on Natural
Religion," that, though every "part" of Nature may be dependent
on other parts for its explanation, the *whole* system of facts or
events which we call Nature may as a whole be self-explanatory;
the "world" itself may be that "necessary being" of which philosophers and divines have spoken. In other words, a complex system
in which every member, taken singly, is temporal, may as a complex be eternal; every member may be incomplete, but the whole
may be complete; every member mutable, but the whole unchanging. Thus, as many philosophers of yesterday and today have said,
the "eternal" would just be the temporal fully understood; there
would be no contrast between Nature and "supernature," but only
between "Nature apprehended as a whole" and Nature as we have
to apprehend her fragmentarily. The thought is a pretty one, but
I cannot believe that it will stand criticism. The very first question
suggested by the sort of formula I have just quoted is whether it
is not actually self-contradictory to call Nature a "whole" at all;
if it is, there can clearly be no apprehending of Nature as something which she is not. And I think it quite clear that Nature, in

---

[4] Or rather, the sceptical critic in the *Dialogues*. We cannot be sure of Hume's
own agreement with the suggestion.

the sense of the complex of events, is, in virtue of her very structure, something incomplete and not a true whole. I can explain the point best, perhaps, by an absurdly simplified example. Let us suppose that Nature consists of just four constituents, A, B, C, D. We are supposed to "explain" the behaviour of A by the structure of B, C, and D, and the interaction of B, C, and D with A, and similarly with each of the other three constituents. Obviously enough, with a set of "general laws" of some kind we can "explain" why A behaves as it does, if we know all about its structure and the structures of B, C, and D. But it still remains entirely unexplained why A should be there at all, or why, if it is there, it should have B, C, and D as its neighbours rather than others with a totally different structure of their own. That this is so has to be accepted as a "brute" fact which is not explained nor yet self-explanatory. Thus no amount of knowledge of "natural laws" will explain the present actual state of Nature unless we also assume it as a brute fact that the distribution of "matter" and "energy" (or whatever else we take as the ultimates of our system of physics) a hundred millions of years ago was such and such. With the same "laws" and a different "initial" distribution the actual state of the world today would be very different. "Collocations," to use Mill's terminology, as well as "laws of causation" have to enter into all our scientific explanations. And though it is true that as our knowledge grows, we are continually learning to assign causes for particular "collocations" originally accepted as bare facts, we only succeed in doing so by falling back on other anterior "collocations" which we have equally to take as unexplained bare facts. As M. Meyerson puts it, we only get rid of the "inexplicable" at one point at the price of introducing it again somewhere else. Now any attempt to treat the complex of facts we call Nature as something which will be found to be more nearly self-explanatory the more of them we know, and would become quite self-explanatory if we only knew them all, amounts to an attempt to eliminate "bare fact" altogether, and reduce Nature simply to a complex of "laws." In other words, it is an attempt to manufacture particular existents out of mere universals, and therefore must end in failure. And the actual progress of science bears witness to this. The more we advance to the reduction of the visible face of Nature to "law," the more, not the less, complex and baffling become the mass of characters which we have to attribute as bare unexplained fact to our ultimate constituents. An electron is a much stiffer dose of "brute" fact than one of Newton's hard impenetrable corpuscles.

Thus we may fairly say that to surrender ourselves to the suggestion that Nature, if we only knew enough, would be seen to be a self-explanatory whole is to follow a will-of-the-wisp. The duality of "law" and "fact" cannot be eliminated from natural science, and this means that in the end either Nature is not explicable at all, or, if she is, the explanation has to be sought in something "outside" on which Nature depends.

(2) Hence it is not surprising that both among men of science and among philosophers there is just now a strong tendency to give up the attempt to "explain" Nature completely and to fall back on an "ultimate pluralism." This means that we resign ourselves to the admission of the duality of "law" and "fact." We assume that there are a plurality of ultimately different constituents of Nature, each with its own specific character and way of behaving, and our business in explanation is simply to show how to account for the world as we find it by the fewest and simplest laws of interaction between these different constituents. In other words we give up altogether the attempt to "explain Nature"; we are content to "explain" lesser "parts" of Nature in terms of their specific character and their relations to other "parts." This is clearly a completely justified mode of procedure for a man of science who is aiming at the solution of some particular problem such as, for example, the discovery of the conditions under which a permanent new "species" originates and maintains itself. But it is quite another question whether "ultimate pluralism" can be the last word of a "philosophy of Nature." If you take it so, it really means that in the end you have no reason to assign why there should be just so many ultimate constituents of "Nature" as you say there are, or why they should have the particular characters you say they have, except that "it happens to be the case." You are acquiescing in unexplained brute fact, not because in the present state of knowledge you do not see your way to do better, but on the plea that there is and can be no

explanation. You are putting unintelligible mystery at the very heart of reality.

Perhaps it may be rejoined, "And why should we not acknowledge this, seeing that, whether we like it or not, we must come to this in the end?" Well, at least it may be retorted that to acquiesce in such a "final inexplicability" as final means that you have denied the validity of the very assumption on which all science is built. All through the history of scientific advance it has been taken for granted that we are not to acquiesce in inexplicable brute fact; whenever we come across what, with our present light, has to be accepted as merely fact, we have a right to ask for further explanation, and should be false to the spirit of science if we did not. Thus we inevitably reach the conclusion that either the very principles which inspire and guide scientific inquiry itself are an illusion, or Nature itself must be dependent on some reality which is self-explanatory, and therefore not Nature nor any part of Nature, but, in the strict sense of the words, "supernatural" or "transcendent"—transcendent, that is, in the sense that in it there is overcome that duality of "law" and "fact" which is characteristic of Nature and every part of Nature. It is not "brute" fact, and yet it is not an abstract universal law or complex of such laws, but a really existing self-luminous Being, such that you could see, if you only apprehended its true character, that to have that character and to be are the same thing. This is the way in which Nature, as it seems to me, inevitably points beyond itself as the temporal and mutable to an "other" which is eternal and immutable.

The "argument from design," rightly stated, seems to me to have a similar force. In our small region of the universe, at any rate, we can see for ourselves that the course of development has taken a very remarkable direction. It has led up, through a line of species which have had to adapt themselves to their "environment," to the emergence of an intelligent and moral creature who adapts his environment to himself and even to his ideals of what he is not yet but ought to be and hopes to be, and the environment of the species he "domesticates" to his own purposes. It is increasingly true as we pass from savagery to civilisation that men make their own environment and are not made by it. On the face of it, it at least looks as though, so far as our own region of Nature is concerned, this emergence of creatures who, being intelligent and moral, freely shape their own environment, is the culminating stage beyond which the development of new species cannot go, and that the whole anterior history of the inorganic and prehuman organic development of our planet has been controlled throughout by the requirements of this "end." I know it will be said that we have no proof that the same thing has happened anywhere else in the "universe"; our planet may, for all we know, not be a fair "average sample." Again, it may be urged that there are reasons for thinking that the history of our planet will end in its unfitness first to contain intelligent human life, and then to contain any form of life; consequently man and all his works cannot be the "end of evolution" even on this earth, but must be a mere passing phase in a process which is controlled by no "ends," and is therefore in no true sense of the term a "history." One would not wish to shirk any of these objections, and yet it is, I think, not too much to say that, to anyone but a fanatical atheist, it will always appear preposterous to regard the production of moral and intelligent masters of Nature as a mere by-product or accident of "evolution on this planet," or indeed as anything but the "end" which has all along determined the process. "Nature," we might say, really does show a "trend" or "bias" to the production of intelligence surpassing her own. And further, we must remember that if there is such a "trend," it will be necessary to include under the head of the processes it determines, not only the emergence of the various forms of prehuman life on our earth, but the "geological" preparation of the earth itself to be the scene of the ensuing development and the preparation during the still remoter astronomical period of the formation of our solar system. Thus to recognise so-called "quasi-purposiveness" even in the course development has followed on "one tiny planet" inevitably involves finding the same quasi-purposiveness on a vaster scale, throughout the whole indefinite range of natural events.[5] The more we are alive to this simple consideration

[5] This is not to say that man is the sole or chief end of Creation, a proposition which, in fact, no orthodox Christian theologian would make; at least not without very careful explanations and reservations. But it is worth while to

that "*de facto* determination by ends," once admitted anywhere in Nature, cannot be confined to any single region or part of Nature but inevitably penetrates everywhere, the more impossible it becomes to be satisfied with such expressions as "quasi-purposive" or "*de facto*" teleology and the like.

The vaster the dominating "plan," the more vividly must it suggest a planning and guiding intelligence. Nature herself, we may suppose (if we allow ourselves to use the miserably misleading personification at all), may, as has been said, be like a sleep-walker who executes trains of purposive acts without knowing that he does so. But the plan itself cannot have originated without a wakeful and alert intelligence. (Even the sleep-walker, as we know, only performs trains of acts adjusted to ends in his sleep because he has first learnt consciously to adjust means to ends in his waking life.) Let "Nature" be as unconscious as you please: the stronger is the suggestion that the marvellous, and often comical, "adaptations" of a highly complex character which pervade "Nature" are the "artifices" of one who neither slumbers nor sleeps. What look like "accidents" may very well be deliberate designs of a master artist, or, as Plato says, contrary to the proverbial expression, it may be Nature which "imitates" Art. I will not attempt to estimate the amount of probative force which ought to be ascribed to these suggestions. It is enough for my purpose that they are there, and that their drawing has notoriously been felt with special intensity by so many of those

---

remind ourselves that there is nothing in itself absurd in the view of the Middle Ages that human history is the central interest, the main plot, of the drama of the universe. For all we *know*, our planet may be the only home of beings "with immortal souls to be saved." If it is, then the fact that it is "*tiny*" is obviously irrelevant as a reason for denying its central importance. When I reflect on the capacities of a man for good and evil, I see nothing ludicrous in the supposition, which, however, I am not making, that it might have been the chief purpose of a wise Creator in making the solar system that the sun should give us men light and warmth.

All I seriously wish to insist on, however, is that to let in "purpose" *anywhere* into natural fact means letting it in *everywhere*. Give it an inch and it will rightly take infinite room. (This as a reply to the arguments based on the allegation that we cannot regard the part of things with which we are acquainted as a "fair average sample." What we are acquainted with is not a definite isolated "part" or "region," but has ramifications which extend indefinitely far.)

who are best acquainted with the facts, even where their meta-physical bias has led them to withhold assent.

The spectacle of movement and change which we call "Nature" thus at least suggests the presence of some "transcendent" source of movement and change which is strictly eternal, being above all mutability and having no succession of phases within itself, and is omnipotent, since it is itself the source of *all* "becoming." The orderliness and apparent purposive "trend towards intelligence" in Nature similarly at least suggest that this omnipotent and eternal "supernatural" is a wholly intelligent Will. The force of the suggestion seems to have been felt by man in every stage of his history so far as that history is accessible to us. It is noteworthy that the more intimate our inquiries become with the "savages" who by our estimate stand nearest to a precivilised condition, the clearer it becomes that even those of them who have been set down on first acquaintance as wholly "godless" turn out, on better knowledge, to have their traditions of a "maker of life" and the like. And at the same time we are not dealing with anything which can be set aside as a "relic of primitive savagery." *Our* conception of "One God the Father Almighty, Creator of heaven and earth," has come to us from two immediate sources, Greek science and philosophy and Hebrew prophecy, and both science and prophecy, as cannot be too often repeated, began by a complete break with the "primitive superstition" of the past. Belief in God as the source of Nature is thus a "survival of primitive superstition" only in the same sense in which the same could be said of belief in causality[6] or, if you prefer it, in "laws of uniform sequence."

So far, however, our attention has been confined to what Bona-ventura calls the "things around and below us," and they clearly have taken us a very little way indeed in the direction of suggesting the reality of a God who is God in the religious man's sense, a being who can be loved and trusted utterly and without qualification. In the creatures we may have discerned the "footprints" of a Cre-ator, but we have seen no token of his "likeness." Perhaps, if we

[6] It is significant that Witgenstein's penetrating though unbalanced *Tractatus logico-philosophicus* definitely *identifies* "superstition" with the belief in caus-ality. *Op. cit.* 5·1361.

turn our attention to "what is within us," we may find in our own moral being the suggestion of something further. We may get at any rate a hint that the creative intelligence we divine behind all things has also the character which makes adoration, love, and trust, as distinguished from mere wonder, possible. In man's moral being we may discern not the mere "footprints" but the "image" of God.

II. FROM MAN TO GOD

With the line of thought we have now to consider we can deal more briefly. If meditation on the creatures in general leads us by a circuitous route and an obscure light to the thought of their Maker, meditation on the moral being of man suggests God more directly and much less obscurely. For we are now starting a fresh stage of the "ascent" from a higher level, and it is with the road to God as with Dante's purgatorial mountain: the higher you have mounted, the easier it is to rise higher still. In Nature we at best see God under a disguise so heavy that it allows us to discern little more than that someone is there; within our own moral life we see Him with the mask, so to say, half fallen off.

Once more the general character of the ascent is the same; we begin with the temporal, and in a certain sense the natural, to end in the eternal and supernatural. But the line of thought, though kindred to the first, is independent, so that Nature and Man are like two witnesses who have had no opportunity of collusion. The clearer and more emphatic testimony of the latter to what was testified less unambiguously by the former affords a further confirmation of our hope that we have read the suggestions of Nature, so ambiguous in their purport, aright.

A single sentence will be enough to show both the analogy of the argument from Man to God with the argument from Nature and the real independence of the two lines of testimony. Nature, we have urged, on inspection points to the "supernatural" beyond itself as its own presupposition; if we look within ourselves we shall see that in man "Nature" and "supernature" meet; he has both within his own heart, and is a denizen at once of the temporal and of the eternal. He has not, like the animals, so far as we can judge of their inner life, one "environment" to which he must adapt himself but two, a secular and an eternal. Because he is designed ultimately to be at home with God in the eternal, he can never be really at home in this world, but at best is, like Abraham, a pilgrim to a promised but unseen land; at worst, like Cain, an aimless fugitive and wanderer on the face of the earth. The very "image" of his Maker which has been stamped on him is not only a sign of his rightful domination over the creatures; it is also "the mark of Cain" from which all creatures shrink. Hence among all the creatures, many of whom are comic enough, man is alone in being tragic. His life, at the very best, is a tragicomedy; at the worst, it is stark tragedy. And naturally enough this is so; for, if man has only the "environment" which is common to him with the beasts of the field, his whole life is no more than a perpetual attempt to find a rational solution of an equation all whose roots are surds. He can only achieve adjustment to one of his two "environments" by sacrifices of adjustment to the other; he can no more be equally in tune with the eternal and the secular at once than a piano can be exactly in tune for all keys. In practice we know how the difficulty is apparently solved in the best human lives; it is solved by cultivating our earthly attachments and yet also practising a high detachment, not "setting our hearts" too much on the best of temporal goods, since "the best in this kind are but shadows," "using" the creatures, but always in the remembrance that the time will come when we can use them no more, loving them but loving them *ordinate,* with care not to lose our hearts to any of them. Wise men do not need to be reminded that the deliberate voluntary refusal of real good things is necessary, as a protection against the overvaluation of the secular, in any life they count worth living. And yet wise men know also that the renunciation of real good which they recommend is not recommended for the mere sake of being without "good." Good is always renounced for the sake of some "better good." But the "better good" plainly cannot be any of the good things of this secular existence. For there is none of them whatever which it may not be a duty to renounce for some man and at some time.

I do not mean merely that occasions demand the sacrifice of the sort of thing the "average sensual man" calls good—comfort, wealth, influence, rank and the like. For no serious moralist would dream of regarding any of these as more, at best, than very inferior goods. I mean that the same thing holds true of the very things to which men of nobler mould are ready to sacrifice these obvious and secondary goods. For example, there are few, if any, earthly goods to compare with our personal affections. Yet a man must be prepared to sacrifice all his personal affections in the service of his country, or for what he honestly believes to be the one Church of God. But there are things to which the greatest lover of his country or his Church must be prepared in turn to sacrifice what lies so near his heart. I may die for my country, I may, as so many a fighting man does, leave wife and young children to run the extreme hazards of fortune, but I must not purchase peace and safety for this country I love so much by procuring the privy murder of a dangerous and remorseless enemy. I may give my body to be burned for my faith, I may leave my little ones to beg their bread for its sake, but I must not help it in its need by a fraud or a forgery. It may be argued that for the good of the human race I ought to be prepared to sacrifice the very independence of my native land, but for no advantage to the whole body of mankind may I insult justice by knowingly giving sentence or verdict against the innocent. If these things are not true, the whole foundation of our morality is dissolved; if they are true, the greatest good, to which I must at need be prepared to sacrifice everything else, must be something which cannot even be appraised in the terms of a secular arithmetic, something incommensurable with the "welfare" of Church and State or even of the whole human race. If it is to be had in fruition at all, it must be had where the secular environment has finally and for ever fallen away, "yonder" as the Neoplatonist would say, "in heaven" as the ordinary Christian says. If this world of time and passage were really our home and our only home, I own I should find it impossible to justify such a complete surrender of all temporal good as that I have spoken of; yet it is certain that the sacrifice is no more than what is demanded, when the need arises, by the most familiar principles of morality. Whoever says "ought," meaning "ought," is in the act bearing witness to the supernatural and supratemporal as the destined home of man. No doubt we should all admit that there are very many rules of our conventional morality which are not of unconditional and universal obligation; we "ought" to conform to them under certain specified and understood conditions. I ought to be generous only when I have first satisfied the just claims of my creditors, just as I ought to abstain from redressing grievances with the high hand when society supplies me with the machinery for getting them redressed by the law. But whoever says "ought" at all, must mean that at least *when* the requisite conditions are fulfilled the obligation is absolute. There may be occasions when it is not binding on me to speak the truth to a questioner, but if there is one single occasion on which I ought to speak the truth, I ought to speak it then, "though the sky should fall."

Now, if there ever is a single occasion on which we ought to speak the truth, or to do anything else, "at all costs" as we say, what is the good in the name of which this unconditional demand is made of me? It cannot be any secular good that can be named, my own health or prosperity or life, nor even the prosperity and pleasurable existence of mankind. For I can never, since the consequences of my act are endless and unforeseeable, be sure that I may not be endangering these very goods by my act, and yet I am sure that the act is one which I ought to do. No doubt, you may fall back upon probability as the guide of life and say, "I ought to do this act because it seems to me most likely to conduce to the temporal well-being of myself, my family, my nation, or my kind." And in practice these are, no doubt, the sort of considerations by which we are constantly influenced. But it should be clear that they cannot be the ultimate grounds of obligation, unless all morality is to be reduced to the status of a convenient illusion. To say that the ultimate ground of an obligation is the mere fact that a man thinks he would further such a concrete tangible end by his act involves the consequence that no man is bound to do any act unless he thinks it will have these results, and that he may do anything he pleases so long as he thinks it will have them. At heart, I believe, even the writers who go furthest in professing to accept these conclusions do themselves a moral injustice. I am convinced that there is not one of them, whatever he may hold in theory, who would not in practice "draw the line" somewhere and say, "This thing I will not do, whatever the cost may be to myself or to anyone else or to everyone." Now an obligation wholly independent of all temporal "consequences" clearly cannot have its justification in the temporal, nor oblige any creature constructed to find his good wholly in the temporal. Only to a being who has in his structure the adaptation to the eternal can you significantly say "You ought."[7]

It will be seen that the thought on which we have dwelt in the last paragraph is one of the underlying fundamental themes of Kant's principal ethical treatise, the "Critique of Practical Reason." It is characteristic of Kant that, wrongly as I think, he wholly distrusted the suggestions of the "supernatural" to be derived from the contemplation of Nature itself, and that, from an exaggerated dread of unregulated fanaticism and superstition, characteristic of his century, he was all but blind to the third source of suggestion of which we have yet to speak. Hence with him it is our knowledge of our own moral being, as creatures who have unconditional obligations, which has to bear the whole weight of the argument. Here, I own, he seems to me to be definitely wrong. The full force of the vindication of religion cannot be felt unless we recognise that its weight is supported not by one strand only but by a cord of three intertwined strands; we need to integrate Bonaventura and Thomas and Butler with Kant to appreciate the real strength of the believer's position. Yet Kant seems to me unquestionably right as far as this. Even were there nothing else to suggest to us that we are denizens at once of a natural and temporal and of a supernatural and eternal world, the revelation of our own inner division against ourselves afforded by Conscience, duly meditated, is enough to bear the strain. Or, to make my point rather differently, I would urge that of all the philosophical thinkers who have concerned themselves with the life of man as a moral being, the two who stand out, even in the estimation of those who dissent from them, as the great undying moralists of literature, Plato and Kant, are just the two who have

---

[7] I owe the expression to a report of a recent utterance of some Roman Catholic divine. I regret that I cannot give the precise reference.

insisted most vigorously on what the secularly minded call, by way of depreciation, the "dualism" of "this world" and the "other world," or, in Kantian language, of "man as (natural) phenomenon" and "man as (supernatural) reality." To deny the reality of this antithesis is to eviscerate morality.

We see this at once if we compare Kant, for example, with Hume, or Plato with Aristotle. It is so obvious that Plato and Kant really "care" about moral practice and Aristotle and Hume do not care, or do not care as much as they ought. In Hume's hands moral goodness is put so completely on a level with mere respectability that our approval of virtue and disapproval of vice is said in so many words to be at bottom one in kind with our preference of a well dressed man to a badly dressed. Aristotle cares more than this. He reduces moral goodness to the discharge of the duties of a good citizen, family man, and neighbour in this secular life, and is careful to insist that these obligations are not to be shirked. But when he comes to speak of the true happiness of man and the kind of life which he lives "as a being with something divine in him," we find that the life of this "divine" part means nothing more than the promotion of science. To live near to God means to him not justice, mercy, and humility, as it does to Plato and the Hebrew prophets, but to be a metaphysician, a physicist, and an astronomer. Justice, mercy, and humility are to be practised, but only for a secular purpose, in order that the man of science may have an orderly and quiet social "environment" and so be free, as he would not be if he had to contend with disorderly passions in himself or his neighbours, to give the maximum of time and interest to the things which really matter. We cannot say of Hume, nor of Aristotle, nor indeed of any moralist who makes morality merely a matter of right social adjustments in this temporal world, what you can say of Plato or Kant, *beati qui esuriunt et sitiunt justitiam.* "Otherworldliness" is as characteristic of the greatest theoretical moralists as it is of all the noblest livers, whatever their professed theories may be.

.   .   .   .

God's Existence as a Postulate of Morality

Immanuel Kant (1724–1804), a German, was one of the most in-fluential modern philosophers. He was noted primarily for his at-tempt to combine the rationalist and the empiricist strains in European philosophy. Major works include *Critique of Pure Reason, Critique of Practical Reason, Critique of Judgment,* and *Prolegomena to Any Future Metaphysics.*

V. THE EXISTENCE OF GOD AS A POSTULATE OF PURE PRACTICAL REASON

In the foregoing analysis the moral law led to a practical problem which is prescribed by pure reason alone, without the aid of any sensible motives, namely, that of the necessary completeness of the first and principal element of the *summum bonum,* namely, Mo-rality; and as this can be perfectly solved only in eternity, to the postulate of *immortality.* The same law must also lead us to affirm the possibility of the second element of the *summum bonum,* namely, Happiness proportioned to that morality, and this on grounds as disinterested as before, and solely from impartial reason; that is, it must lead to the supposition of the existence of a cause

* From I. Kant, *Critique of Practical Reason,* tr. by T. K. Abbott.

adequate to this effect; in other words, it must postulate the *existence of God,* as the necessary condition of the possibility of the *summum bonum* (an object of the will which is necessarily connected with the moral legislation of pure reason). We proceed to exhibit this connexion in a convincing manner.

Happiness is the condition of a rational being in the world with whom *everything goes according to his wish and will;* it rests therefore, on the harmony of physical nature with his whole end, and likewise with the essential determining principle of his will. Now the moral law as a law of freedom commands by determining principles, which ought to be quite independent on nature and on its harmony with our faculty of desire (as springs). But the acting rational being in the world is not the cause of the world and of nature itself. There is not the least ground, therefore, in the moral law for a necessary connexion between morality and proportionate happiness in a being that belongs to the world as part of it, and therefore dependent on it, and which for that reason cannot by his will be a cause of this nature, nor by his own power make it thoroughly harmonize, as far as his happiness is concerned, with his practical principles. Nevertheless, in the practical problem of pure reason, that is, the necessary pursuit of the *summum bonum,* such a connexion is postulated as necessary: we ought to endeavour to promote the *summum bonum,* which, therefore, must be possible. Accordingly, the existence of a cause of all nature, distinct from nature itself, and containing the principle of this connexion, namely, of the exact harmony of happiness with morality, is also *postulated.* Now, this supreme cause must contain the principle of the harmony of nature, not merely with a law of the will of rational beings, but with the conception of this *law,* in so far as they make it the *supreme determining principle of the will,* and consequently not merely with the form of morals, but with their morality as their motive, that is, with their moral character. Therefore, the *summum bonum* is possible in the world only on the supposition of a Supreme Being having a causality corresponding to moral character. Now a being that is capable of acting on the conception of laws is an *intelligence* (a rational being), and the causality of such a being according to this conception of laws is his *will;* therefore the supreme cause of nature, which must be presupposed as a condition of the *summum bonum* is a being which is the cause of nature by *intelligence* and *will,* consequently its author, that is God. It follows that the postulate of the possibility of the *highest derived good* (the best world) is likewise the postulate of the reality of a *highest original good,* that is to say, of the existence of God. Now it was seen to be a duty for us to promote the *summum bonum;* consequently it is not merely allowable, but it is a necessity connected with duty as a requisite, that we should presuppose the possibility of this *summum bonum;* and as this is possible only on condition of the existence of God, it inseparably connects the supposition of this with duty; that is, it is morally necessary to assume the existence of God.

It must be remarked here that this moral necessity is *subjective,* that is, it is a want, and not *objective,* that is, itself a duty, for there cannot be a duty to suppose the existence of anything (since this concerns only the theoretical employment of reason). Moreover, it is not meant by this that it is necessary to suppose the existence of God *as a basis of all obligation in general* (for this rests, as has been sufficiently proved, simply on the autonomy of reason itself). What belongs to duty here is only the endeavour to realize and promote the *summum bonum* in the world, the possibility of which can therefore be postulated; and as our reason finds it not conceivable except on the supposition of a supreme intelligence, the admission of this existence is therefore connected with the consciousness of our duty, although the admission itself belongs to the domain of speculative reason. Considered in respect of this alone, as a principle of explanation, it may be called a *hypothesis,* but in reference to the intelligibility of an object given us by the moral law (the *summum bonum*), and consequently of a requirement for practical purposes, it may be called *faith,* that is to say a pure *rational faith,* since pure reason (both in its theoretical and its practical use) is the sole source from which it springs.

From this *deduction* it is now intelligible why the *Greek* schools could never attain the solution of their problem of the practical possibility of the *summum bonum,* because they made the rule of the use which the will of man makes of his freedom the sole and sufficient ground of this possibility, thinking that they had no need for that purpose of the existence of God. No doubt they were so far right that they established the principle of morals of itself independently on this postulate, from the relation of reason only to the will, and consequently made it the *supreme* practical condition of the *summum bonum;* but it was not therefore the *whole* condition of its possibility. The *Epicureans* had indeed assumed as the supreme principle of morality a wholly false one, namely, that of happiness, and had substituted for a law a maxim of arbitrary choice according to every man's inclination; they proceeded, however, *consistently* enough in this, that they degraded their *summum bonum* likewise just in proportion to the meanness of their fundamental principle, and looked for no greater happiness than can be attained by human prudence (including temperance and moderation of the inclinations), and this, as we know, would be scanty enough and would be very different according to circumstances; not to mention the exceptions that their maxims must perpetually admit and which make them incapable of being laws. The *Stoics,* on the contrary, had chosen their supreme practical principle quite rightly, making virtue the condition of the *summum bonum;* but when they represented the degree of virtue required by its pure law as fully attainable in this life, they not only strained the moral powers of the *man* whom they called *the wise* beyond all the limits of his nature, and assumed a thing that contradicts all our knowledge of men, but also and principally they would not allow the second *element* of the *summum bonum,* namely, happiness, to be properly a special object of human desire, but made their *wise man,* like a divinity in his consciousness of the excellence of his person, wholly independent on nature (as regards his own contentment); they exposed him indeed to the evils of life, but made him not subject to them (at the same time representing him also as free from moral evil). They thus, in fact, left out the second element of the *summum bonum,* namely personal happiness, placing it solely in action and satisfaction with one's own personal worth, thus including it in the consciousness of being morally minded, in which they might have been sufficiently refuted by the voice of their own nature.

The doctrine of Christianity,[1] even if we do not yet consider it as a religious doctrine, gives, touching this point, a conception of the *summum bonum* (the kingdom of God), which alone satisfies the strictest demand of practical reason. The moral law is holy (unyielding) and demands holiness of morals, although all the moral perfection to which man can attain is still only virtue, that is, a rightful disposition arising from *respect* for the law, implying consciousness of a constant propensity to transgression, or at least a want of purity, that is, a mixture of many spurious (not moral) motives of obedience to the law, consequently a self-esteem combined with humility. In respect, then, of the holiness which the Christian law requires, this leaves the creature nothing but a

[1] It is commonly held that the Christian precept of morality has no advantage in respect of purity over the moral conceptions of the Stoics; the distinction between them is, however, very obvious. The Stoic system made the consciousness of strength of mind the pivot on which all moral dispositions should turn; and although its disciples spoke of duties and even defined them very well, yet they placed the spring and proper determining principle of the will in an elevation of the mind above the lower springs of the senses, which owe their power only to weakness of mind. With them, therefore, virtue was a sort of heroism in the *wise man* who, raising himself above the animal nature of man, is sufficient for himself, and while he prescribes duties to others is himself raised above them, and is not subject to any temptation to transgress the moral law. All this, however, they could not have done if they had conceived this law in all its purity and strictness, as the precept of the Gospel does. When I give the name *idea* to a perfection to which nothing adequate can be given in experience, it does not follow that the moral ideas are something transcendent, that is something of which we could not even determine the concept adequately, or of which it is uncertain whether there is any object corresponding to it at all, as is the case with the ideas of speculative reason; on the contrary, being types of practical perfection, they serve as the indispensable rule of conduct and likewise as the *standard of comparison*. Now if I consider *Christian morals* on their philosophical side, then compared with the ideas of the Greek schools they would appear as follows: the ideas of the *Cynics*, the *Epicureans*, the *Stoics*, and the *Christians* are: *simplicity of nature, prudence, wisdom*, and *holiness*. In respect of the way of attaining them, the Greek schools were distinguished from one another thus, that the Cynics only required *common sense*, the others the path of *science*, but both found the mere *use of natural powers* sufficient for the purpose. Christian morality, because its precept is framed (as a moral precept must be) so pure and unyielding, takes from man all confidence that he can be fully adequate to it, at least in this life, but again sets it up by enabling us to hope that if we act as well as it is in our *power* to do, then what is not in our power will come in to our aid from another source, whether we know how this may be or not. *Aristotle* and *Plato* differed only as to the *origin* of our moral conceptions.

progress *in infinitum,* but for that very reason it justifies him in hoping for an endless duration of his existence. The *worth* of a character *perfectly* accordant with the moral law is infinite, since the only restriction on all possible happiness in the judgment of a wise and all-powerful distributor of it is the absence of conformity of rational beings to their duty. But the moral law of itself does not *promise* any happiness, for according to our conceptions of an order of nature in general, this is not necessarily connected with obedience to the law. Now Christian morality supplies this defect (of the second indispensable element of the *summum bonum*) by representing the world, in which rational beings devote themselves with all their soul to the moral law, as a *kingdom of God,* in which nature and morality are brought into a harmony foreign to each of itself, by a holy Author who makes the derived *summum bonum* possible. *Holiness* of life is prescribed to them as a rule even in this life, while the welfare proportioned to it, namely, *bliss,* is represented as attainable only in an eternity; because the *former* must always be the pattern of their conduct in every state, and progress towards it is already possible and necessary in this life; while the *latter,* under the name of happiness, cannot be attained at all in this world (so far as our own power is concerned), and therefore is made simply an object of hope. Nevertheless, the Christian principle of *morality* itself is not theological (so as to be heteronomy), but is autonomy of pure practical reason, since it does not make the knowledge of God and His will the foundation of these laws, but only of the attainment of the *summum bonum,* on condition of following these laws, and it does not even place the proper *spring* of this obedience in the desired results, but solely in the conception of duty, as that of which the faithful observance alone constitutes the worthiness to obtain those happy consequences.

In this manner the moral laws lead through the conception of the *summum bonum* as the object and final end of pure practical reason to *religion,* that is, to the *recognition of all duties as divine commands, not as sanctions, that is to say, arbitrary ordinances of a foreign will and contingent in themselves,* but as essential *laws* of every free will in itself, which, nevertheless, must be regarded as commands of the Supreme Being, because it is only from a morally perfect (holy and good) and at the same time all-powerful will, and consequently only through harmony with this will, that we can hope to attain the *summum bonum* which the moral law makes it our duty to take as the object of our endeavours. Here again, then, all remains disinterested and founded merely on duty; neither fear nor hope being made the fundamental springs, which if taken as principles would destroy the whole moral worth of actions. The moral law commands me to make the highest possible good in a world the ultimate object of all my conduct. But I cannot hope to effect this otherwise than by the harmony of my will with that of a holy and good Author of the world; and although the conception of the *summum bonum* as a whole, in which the greatest happiness is conceived as combined in the most exact proportion with the highest degree of moral perfection (possible in creatures), includes *my own happiness,* yet it is not this that is the determining principle of the will which is enjoined to promote the *summum bonum,* but the moral law, which, on the contrary, limits by strict conditions my unbounded desire of happiness.

Hence also morality is not properly the doctrine how we should *make* ourselves happy, but how we should become *worthy* of happiness. It is only when religion is added that there also comes in the hope of participating some day in happiness in proportion as we have endeavoured to be not unworthy of it.

A man is *worthy* to possess a thing or a state when his possession of it is in harmony with the *summum bonum.* We can now easily see that all worthiness depends on moral conduct, since in the conception of the *summum bonum* this constitutes the condition of the rest (which belongs to one's state), namely, the participation of happiness. Now it follows from this that *morality* should never be treated as a *doctrine of happiness,* that is, an instruction how to become happy; for it has to do simply with the rational condition (*conditio sine qua non*) of happiness, not with the means of attaining it. But when morality has been completely expounded (which merely imposes duties instead of providing rules for selfish desires), then first, after the moral desire to promote the *summum bonum* (to bring the kingdom of God to us) has been awakened, a desire founded on a law, and which could not previously arise in any selfish mind, and when for the behoof of this desire the step to religion has been taken, then this ethical doctrine may be also called a doctrine of happiness because the *hope* of happiness first begins with religion only.

We can also see from this that, when we ask what is *God's ultimate end* in creating the world, we must not name the *happiness* of the rational beings in it, but the *summum bonum,* which adds a further condition to that wish of such beings, namely, the condition of being worthy of happiness, that is, the *morality* of these same rational beings, a condition which alone contains the rule by which only they can hope to share in the former at the hand of a *wise* Author. For as *wisdom* theoretically considered signifies *the knowledge of the summum bonum,* and practically *the accordance of the will with the summum bonum,* we cannot attribute to a supreme independent wisdom an end based merely on *goodness.* For we cannot conceive the action of this goodness (in respect of the happiness of rational beings) as suitable to the highest original good, except under the restrictive conditions of harmony with the holiness[2] of His will. Therefore those who placed the end of creation in the glory of God (provided that this is not conceived anthropomorphically as a desire to be praised) have perhaps hit upon the best expression. For nothing glorifies God more than that which is the most estimable thing in the world, respect for His command, the observance of the holy duty that His law imposes on us, when there is added thereto His glorious plan of crowning such a beautiful order of things with corresponding happiness. If the latter (to speak humanly) make Him worthy of love, by the *former* He is an

[2] In order to make these characteristics of these conceptions clear, I add the remark that whilst we ascribe to God various attributes, the quality of which we also find applicable to creatures, only that in Him they are raised to the highest degree, *e.g.* power, knowledge, presence, goodness, etc., under the designations of omnipotence, omniscience, omnipresence, etc., there are three that are ascribed to God exclusively, and yet without the addition of greatness, and which are all moral. He is the *only holy,* the *only blessed,* the *only wise,* because these conceptions already imply the absence of limitation. In the order of these attributes He is also the *holy lawgiver* (and creator), the *good governor* (and preserver), and the *just judge,* three attributes which include everything by which God is the object of religion, and in conformity with which the metaphysical perfections are added of themselves in the reason.

object of adoration. Even men can never acquire respect by benevolence alone, though they may gain love, so that the greatest beneficence only procures them honour when it is regulated by worthiness.

That in the order of ends, man (and with him every rational being) is *an end in himself*, that is, that he can never be used merely as a means by any (not even by God) without being at the same time an end also himself, that therefore *humanity* in our person must be *holy* to ourselves, this follows now of itself because he is the *subject of the moral law*, in other words, of that which is holy in itself, and on account of which and in agreement with which alone can anything be termed holy. For this moral law is founded on the autonomy of his will, as a free will which by its universal laws must necessarily be able to agree with that to which it is to submit itself.

VI. OF THE POSTULATES OF PURE PRACTICAL REASON IN GENERAL

They all proceed from the principle of morality, which is not a postulate but a law, by which reason determines the will directly, which will, because it is so determined as a pure will, requires these necessary conditions of obedience to its precept. These postulates are not theoretical dogmas but, suppositions practically necessary; while then they do [not] extend our speculative knowledge, they give objective reality to the ideas of speculative reason in general (by means of their reference to what is practical), and give it a right to concepts, the possibility even of which it could not otherwise venture to affirm.

These postulates are those *of immortality, freedom* positively considered (as the causality of a being so far as he belongs to the intelligible world), and the *existence of God*. The *first* results from the practically necessary condition of a duration adequate to the complete fulfilment of the moral law; the *second* from the necessary supposition of independence on the sensible world, and of the faculty of determining one's will according to the law of an intelligible world, that is, of freedom; the *third* from the necessary condition of the existence of the *summum bonum* in such an intelligible world, by the supposition of the supreme independent good, that is, the existence of God.

Thus the fact that respect for the moral law necessarily makes the *summum bonum* an object of our endeavours, and the supposition thence resulting of its objective reality, lead through the postulates of practical reason to conceptions which speculative reason might indeed present as problems, but could never solve. Thus it leads: (1) To that one in the solution of which the latter could do nothing but commit *paralogisms* (namely, that of immortality), because it could not lay hold of the character of permanence, by which to complete the psychological conception of an ultimate subject necessarily ascribed to the soul in self-consciousness, so as to make it the real conception of a substance, a character which practical reason furnishes by the postulate of a duration required for accordance with the moral law in the *summum bonum,* which is the whole end of practical reason. (2) It leads to that of which speculative reason contained nothing but *antinomy,* the solution of which it could only found on a notion problematically conceivable indeed, but whose objective reality it could not prove or determine, namely, the *cosmological* idea of an intelligible world and the consciousness of our existence in it, by means of the postulate of freedom (the reality of which it lays down by virtue of the moral law), and with it likewise the law of an intelligible world, to which speculative reason could only point, but could not define its conception. (3) What speculative reason was able to think, but was obliged to leave undetermined as a mere transcendental *ideal,* namely, the *theological* conception of the First Being, to this it gives significance (in a practical view, that is, as a condition of the possibility of the object of a will determined by that law), namely, as the supreme principle of the *summum bonum* in an intelligible world, by means of moral legislation in it invested with sovereign power.

Is our knowledge, however, actually extended in this way by pure practical reason, and is that *immanent* in practical reason which for the speculative was only *transcendent?* Certainly, but *only in a practical point of view.* For we do not thereby take knowledge of the nature of our souls, nor of the intelligible world, nor of the Supreme Being, with respect to what they are in themselves, but we have merely combined the conceptions of them in the *practical* concept of the *summum bonum* as the object of our will, and this altogether *à priori*, but only by means of the moral law, and merely in reference to it, in respect of the object which it commands. But how freedom is possible, and how we are to conceive this kind of causality theoretically and positively, is not thereby discovered; but only that there is such a causality is postulated by the moral law and in its behoof. It is the same with the remaining ideas, the possibility of which no human intelligence will ever fathom, but the truth of which, on the other hand, no sophistry will ever wrest from the conviction even of the commonest man.

J. J. C. SMART

The Existence of God

J. J. C. Smart (1920–   ) is a contemporary Australian philosopher.

This lecture[1] is not to discuss whether God exists. It is to discuss reasons which philosophers have given for saying that God exists. That is, to discuss certain arguments.

First of all it may be as well to say what we may hope to get out of this. Of course, if we found that any of the traditional arguments for the existence of God were sound, we should get out of our one hour this Sunday afternoon something of inestimable value, such as one never got out of any hours' work in our lives before. For we should have got out of one hour's work the answer to that question about which, above all, we want to know the answer. (This is assuming for the moment that the question "Does God exist?" is a proper question. The fact that a question is all right as far as the rules of ordinary grammar are concerned does

*From J. J. C. Smart, "The Existence of God," in A. Flew and A. MacIntyre, eds., *New Essays in Philosophical Theology*. (First published in *The Church Quarterly Review*, 1955). Reprinted with the permission of J. J. C. Smart, and SCM Press, Ltd., and The Macmillan Company.

[1] A public lecture given at the University of Adelaide in 1951.

not ensure that it has a sense. For example, "Does virtue run faster than length?" is certainly all right as far as ordinary grammar is concerned, but it is obviously not a meaningful question. Again, "How fast does time flow?" is all right as far as ordinary grammar is concerned, but it has no clear meaning. Now some philosophers would ask whether the question "Does God exist?" is a proper question. The greatest danger to theism at the present moment does not come from people who deny the validity of the arguments for the existence of God, for many Christian theologians do not believe that the existence of God can be proved, and certainly nowhere in the Old or New Testaments do we find any evidence of people's religion having a metaphysical basis. The main danger to theism today comes from people who want to say that "God exists" and "God does not exist" are equally absurd. The concept of God, they would say, is a nonsensical one. Now I myself shall later give grounds for thinking that the question "Does God exist?" is not, in the full sense, a proper question, but I shall also give grounds for believing that to admit this is not necessarily to endanger theology.)

However, let us assume for the moment that the question "Does God exist?" is a proper question. We now ask: Can a study of the traditional proofs of the existence of God enable us to give an affirmative answer to this question? I contend that it can not. I shall point out what seem to me to be fallacies in the main traditional arguments for the existence of God. Does proving that the arguments are invalid prove that God does not exist? Not at all. For to say that an argument is invalid is by no means the same thing as to say that its conclusion is false. Still, if we do find that the arguments we consider are all fallacious, what do we *gain* out of our investigation? Well, one thing we gain is a juster (if more austere) view of what philosophical argument can do for us. But, more important, we get a deeper insight into the logical nature of certain concepts, in particular, of course, the concepts of deity and existence. Furthermore we shall get some hints as to whether philosophy can be of any service to theologians, and if it can be of service, some hints as to how it can be of service. I think that it can be, but I must warn you that many, indeed perhaps the majority, of philosophers today would not entirely agree with me here.

One very noteworthy feature which must strike anyone who first looks at the usual arguments for the existence of God is the extreme brevity of these arguments. They range from a few lines to a few pages. St. Thomas Aquinas presents five arguments in three pages! Would it not be rather extraordinary if such a great conclusion should be got so easily? Before going on to discuss any of the traditional arguments in detail I want to give general grounds for suspecting anyone who claims to settle a controversial question by means of a short snappy argument.

My reason for doubting whether a short snappy argument can ever settle any controversial question is as follows: *any argument can be reversed.* Let me explain this. A question of elementary logic is involved. Let us consider an argument from two premisses, p, q, to a conclusion r:

$$p$$
$$\frac{q}{r}$$

If the argument is valid, that is, if r really does follow from p and q, the argument will lead to agreement about r provided that there already is agreement about p and q. For example, if we have the premisses

p All A, B and C grade cricketers are entitled to a free pass to the Adelaide Oval for Test matches, Sheffield Shield matches, and so forth (quite uncontroversial, it can be got from the rules of the South Australian Cricket Association).

q John Wilkin is an A, B or C grade cricketer. (Quite uncontroversial, everyone knows it.)

we may conclude

r John Wilkin is entitled to a free pass to the Adelaide Oval for Test matches, Sheffield Shield matches, and so forth.

But we now consider this argument:[2]

[2] I owe this illustration, and the whole application to the idea of "reversing the argument," to Prof. D. A. T. Gasking of Melbourne.

p Nothing can come into existence except through the activity of some previously existing thing or being.

q The world had a beginning in time.

therefore

r The world came into existence through the activity of some previously existing thing or being.

If this argument is valid (as it certainly is) then it is equally the case that

(not-*r*) The world did not come into existence through the activity of some previously existing thing or being

implies that either

(not-*p*) Something *can* come into existence otherwise than through the activity of a previously existing thing or being

or

(not-*q*) The world had no beginning in time.

That is, if $\frac{p}{q}$ is valid $\frac{\text{not-}r}{q}$ and $\frac{\text{not-}r}{p}$ must be equally valid.

Now it is possible that a person might think that we have *fewer* reasons for believing *r* than we have for believing (not-*p*) or (not-*q*).

In which case the argument $\frac{p}{q}$ though perfectly valid will not con-

vince him. For he will be inclined to argue in the opposite direction, that is, from the falsity of *r* to the falsity of either *p* or *q*.

This last example is perhaps itself a—not very good—argument for the existence of God, but I have given it purely as an example to show *one* of the things to look out for when criticizing more serious arguments. The other thing to look out for, of course, is whether the argument is *valid*. It is my belief that in the case of any metaphysical argument it will be found that if the premisses are uncontroversial the argument is unfortunately not valid, and that if the argument is valid the premises will unfortunately be just as doubtful as the conclusion they are meant to support.

With these warnings in mind let us proceed to the discussion of the three most famous arguments for the existence of God. These are:

1. The Ontological Argument.
2. The Cosmological Argument.
3. The Teleological Argument.

The first argument—the ontological argument—really has no premises at all. It tries to show that there would be a contradiction in denying that God exists. It was first formulated by St. Anselm and was later used by Descartes. It is not a convincing argument to modern ears, and St. Thomas Aquinas gave essentially the right reasons for rejecting it. However, it is important to discuss it, as an understanding of what is wrong with it is necessary for evaluating the second argument, that is, the cosmological argument. This argument does have a premiss, but not at all a controversial one. It is that something exists. We should all, I think, agree to that. The teleological argument is less austere in manner than the other two. It tries to argue to the existence of God not purely *a priori* and not from the mere fact of *something* existing, but from the actual features we observe in nature, namely those which seem to be evidence of design or purpose.

We shall discuss these three arguments in order. I do not say that they are the only arguments which have been propounded for the existence of God, but they are, I think, the most important ones. For example, of St. Thomas Aquinas' celebrated "Five Ways" the first three are variants of the cosmological argument, and the fifth is a form of the teleological argument.

The Ontological Argument. This as I remarked, contains no factual premiss. It is a *reductio-ad-absurdum* of the supposition that God does not exist. Now *reductio-ad-absurdum* proofs are to be suspected whenever there is doubt as to whether the statement to be proved is *significant.* For example, it is quite easy, as anyone who is familiar with the so-called Logical Paradoxes will know, to produce a not *obviously* nonsensical statement, such that both it *and* its denial imply a contradiction. So unless we are sure of the significance of a statement we cannot regard a *reductio-ad-absurdum* of its contradictory as proving its truth. This point of view is well known to those versed in the philosophy of mathematics; there is a well-known school of mathematicians, led by Brouwer, who refuse in certain circumstances to employ *reductio-ad-absurdum* proofs. However, I shall not press this criticism of the ontological argument, for this criticism is somewhat abstruse (though it has been foreshadowed by Catholic philosophers, who object to the ontological argument by saying that it does not first show that the concept of an infinitely perfect being is a *possible* one). We are at present assuming that "Does God exist?" is a proper question, and if it is a proper question there is no objection so far to answering it by means of a *reductio-ad-absurdum* proof. We shall content ourselves with the more usual criticisms of the ontological argument.

The ontological argument was made famous by Descartes. It is to be found at the beginning of his Fifth Meditation. As I remarked earlier it was originally put forward by Anselm, though I am sorry to say that to read Descartes you would never suspect that fact! Descartes points out that in mathematics we can deduce various things purely *a priori*, "as for example," he says, "when I imagine a triangle, although there is not and perhaps never was in any place . . . one such figure, it remains true nevertheless that this figure possesses a certain determinate nature, form, or essence, which is . . . not framed by me, nor in any degree dependent on my thought; as appears from the circumstance, that diverse properties of the triangle may be demonstrated, for example that its three angles are equal to two right, that its greatest side is subtended by its greatest angle, and the like." Descartes now goes on to suggest that just as having the sum of its angles equal to two right angles is involved in the idea of a triangle, so *existence* is involved in the very idea of an infinitely perfect being, and that it would therefore be as much of a contradiction to assert that an infinitely perfect being does not exist as it is to assert that the three angles of a triangle do not add up to two right angles or that two of its sides are not together greater than the third side. We may then, says Descartes, assert that an infinitely perfect being *necessarily* exists, just as we may say that two sides of a triangle are together *necessarily* greater than the third side.

This argument is highly fallacious. To say that a so-and-so exists is not in the least like saying that a so-and-so has such-and-such a property. It is not to amplify a concept but to say that a concept applies to something, and whether or not a concept applies to something can not be seen from an examination of the concept itself. Existence is not a property. "Growling" is a property of tigers, and to say that "tame tigers growl" is to say something about tame tigers, but to say "tame tigers exist" is not to say something about tame tigers but say that there are tame tigers. Prof. G. E. Moore once brought out the difference between existence and a property such as that of being tame, or being a tiger, or being a growler, by reminding us that though the sentence "some tame tigers do not *growl*" makes perfect sense, the sentence "some tame tigers do not *exist*" has no clear meaning. The fundamental mistake in the ontological argument, then, is that it treats "exists" in "an infinitely perfect being exists" as if it ascribed a property existence to an infinitely perfect being, just as "is loving" in "an infinitely perfect being is loving" ascribes a property, or as "growl" in "tame tigers growl" ascribes a property: the verb "to exist" in "an infinitely perfect being exists" does not ascribe a property to something already conceived of as existing but says that the concept of an infinitely perfect being applies to something. The verb "to exist" here takes us right out of the purely conceptual world. This being so, there can never be any *logical contradiction* in denying that God exists. It is worth mentioning that we are less likely to make the sort of mistake that the ontological argument makes if we use the expression "there is a so-and-so" instead of the more misleading form of words "a so-and-so exists."

I should like to mention another interesting, though less crucial, objection to Descartes' argument. He talks as though you can deduce further properties of, say, a triangle, by considering its definition. It is worth pointing out that from the definition of a triangle as a figure bounded by three straight lines you can only deduce trivialities, such as that it is bounded by more than one straight line, for example. It is not at all a contradiction to say that the two sides of a triangle are together not greater than the third side, or that its angles do not add up to two right angles. To get a contradiction you have to bring in the specific axioms of Euclidean geometry. (Remember school geometry, how you used to prove that the angles of a triangle add up to two right angles. Through the vertex C of the triangle ABC you drew a line parallel to BA, and so you assumed the axiom of parallels for a start.) Definitions, by themselves, are not deductively potent. Descartes, though a very great mathematician himself, was profoundly mistaken as to the nature of mathematics. However, we can interpret him as saying that from the definition of a triangle, *together with the axioms of Euclidean geometry,* you can deduce various things, such as that the angles of a triangle add up to two right angles. But this just shows how pure mathematics is a sort of game with symbols; you start with a set of axioms, and operate on them in accordance with certain rules of inference. All the mathematician requires is that the axiom set should be *consistent.* Whether or not it has application to reality lies outside pure mathematics. Geometry is no fit model for a proof of real existence.

We now turn to the *Cosmological Argument.* This argument does at least seem more promising than the ontological argument. It does start with a factual premiss, namely that something exists. The premiss that something exists is indeed a very abstract one, but nevertheless it *is* factual, it does give us a foothold in the real world of things, it does go beyond the consideration of mere concepts. The argument has been put forward in various forms, but for present purposes it may be put as follows:

Everything in the world around us is *contingent.* That is, with regard to any particular thing, it is quite conceivable that it might not have existed. For example, if you were asked why you existed, you could say that it was because of your parents, and if asked why they existed you could go still further back, but however far you go back you have not, so it is argued, made the fact of your existence really intelligible. For however far back you go in such a series you only get back to something which itself might not have existed. For a really satisfying explanation of why anything contingent (such as you or me or this table) exists you must eventually begin with something which is not itself contingent, that is, with something of which we cannot say that it might not have existed, that is we must begin with a necessary being. So the first part of the argument boils down to this. *If anything exists an absolutely necessary being must exist. Something exists. Therefore an absolutely necessary being must exist.*

The second part of the argument is to prove that a necessarily existing being must be an infinitely perfect being, that is, God. Kant[3] contended that this second stage of the argument is just the ontological argument over again, and of course if this were so the cosmological argument would plainly be a fraud; it begins happily enough with an existential premiss ("something exists") but this would only be a cover for the subsequent employment of the ontological argument. This criticism of Kant's has been generally accepted but I think that certain Thomist philosophers have been right in attributing to Kant's own criticism a mistake in elementary logic. Let us look at Kant's criticism. Kant says, correctly enough, that the conclusion of the second stage of the cosmological argument is "All necessarily existing beings are infinitely perfect beings." This, he says, implies that "Some infinitely perfect beings are necessarily existing beings." Since, however, there could be only one infinitely perfect, unlimited, being, we may replace the proposition "Some infinitely perfect beings are necessarily existing beings" by the proposition "All infinitely perfect beings are necessarily existing beings." (To make this last point clearer let me take an analogous example. If it is true that some men who are Prime Minister of Australia are liberals and if it is also true that there is only one Prime Minister of Australia, then we can equally well say that all men who are Prime Minister of Australia are Liberals. For "some" means "at least one," and if there is only one Prime Minister, then "at least one" is equivalent to "one," which in this case is "all.") So the conclusion of the second stage of the cosmological argument is that "all infinitely perfect beings are necessarily existing beings." This, however, is the principle of the ontological argument, which we have already criticized, and which, for that matter, proponents of the cosmological argument like Thomas Aquinas themselves reject.

Kant has, however, made a very simple mistake. He has forgotten that the existence of a necessary being has already been proved (or thought to have been proved) in the first part of the argument. He changes "All necessary beings are infinitely perfect beings" round to "Some infinitely perfect beings are necessary beings." If this change round is to be valid the existence of a necessary being is already presupposed. Kant has been misled by an ambiguity in "all." "All X's are Y's" may take it for granted that there are some X's or it may not. For example if I say, "All the people in this room are interested in Philosophy," it is already agreed that there are some people in this room. So we can infer that "Some of the people interested in Philosophy are people in this room." So "All the people in this room are interested in Philosophy" says more than "If anyone were in this room he would be interested in Philosophy," for this would be true even if there were in fact no people in this room. (As I wrote this lecture I was quite sure that *if* anyone came he would be interested in Philosophy, and I could have been quite sure of this even if I had doubted whether anyone would come.) Now sometimes "All X's are Y's" does mean only "If anything is an X it is a Y." Take the sentence "All trespassers will be prosecuted." This does not imply that some prosecuted people will be trespassers, for it does not imply that there are or will be any trespassers. Indeed the object of putting it on a notice is to make it more likely that there won't be any trespassers. All that "All trespassers will be prosecuted" says is, "If anyone is a trespasser then he will be prosecuted." So Kant's criticism won't do. He has taken himself and other people in by using "all" sometimes in the one way and sometimes in the other.

While agreeing thus far with Thomist critics of Kant[4] I still want to assert that the cosmological argument is radically unsound. The trouble comes much earlier than where Kant locates it. The trouble

---

[4] See, for example, Fr. T. A. Johnston, *Australasian Journal of Philosophy*, Vol. XXI, pp. 14–15, or D. J. B. Hawkins, *Essentials of Theism*, pp. 67–70, and the review of Fr. Hawkins' book by A. Donagan, *Australasian Journal of Philosophy*, Vol. XXVIII, especially p. 129.

comes in the *first* stage of the argument. For the first stage of the argument purports to argue to the existence of a necessary being. And by "a necessary being" the cosmological argument means "a *logically* necessary being," that is, "a being whose nonexistence is inconceivable in the sort of way that a triangle's having four sides is inconceivable." The trouble is, however, that the concept of a logically necessary being is a self-contradictory concept, like the concept of a round square. For in the first place "necessary" is a predicate of *propositions,* not of things. That is, we can contrast *necessary* propositions such as "3 + 2 = 5," "a thing cannot be red and green all over," "either it is raining or it is not raining," with *contingent* propositions, such as "Mr. Menzies is Prime Minister of Australia," "the earth is slightly flattened at the poles," and "sugar is soluble in water." The propositions in the first class are guaranteed solely by the rules for the use of the symbols they contain. In the case of the propositions of the second class a genuine possibility of agreeing or not agreeing with reality is left open; whether they are true or false depends not on the conventions of our language but on reality. (Compare the contrast between "the equator is 90 degrees from the pole." which tells us nothing about geography but only about our map-making conventions, and "Adelaide is 55 degrees from the pole," which does tell us a geographical fact.) So no informative proposition can be logically necessary. Now since "necessary" is a word which applies primarily to propositions, we shall have to interpret "God is a necessary being" as "The proposition 'God exists' is logically necessary." But this *is* the principle of the ontological argument, and there is no way of getting round it this time in the way that we got out of Kant's criticism. No existential proposition can be logically necessary, for we saw that the truth of a logically necessary proposition depends only on our symbolism, or to put the same thing in another way, on the relationship of concepts. We saw, however, in discussing the ontological argument, that an existential proposition does not say that one concept is involved in another, but that a concept applies to something. An existential proposition must be very different from any logically necessary one, such as a mathematical one, for example, for the conventions of our symbolism clearly leave it open for us either to affirm or deny an existential proposition; it is not our symbolism but reality which decides whether or not we must affirm it or deny it.

The demand that the existence of God should be *logically* necessary is thus a self-contradictory one. When we see this and go back to look at the first stage of the cosmological argument it no longer seems compelling, indeed it now seems to contain an absurdity. If we cast our minds back, we recall that the argument was as follows: that if we explain why something exists and is what it is, we must explain it by reference to something else, and we must explain that thing's being what it is by reference to yet another thing, and so on, back and back. It is then suggested that unless we can go back to a logically necessary first cause we shall remain intellectually unsatisfied. We should otherwise only get back to something which might have been otherwise, and with reference to which the same questions can again be asked. This is the argument, but we now see that in asking for a logically necessary first cause we are doing something worse than asking for the moon. It is only *physically* impossible for us to get the moon; if I were a few million times bigger I could reach out for it and give it to you. That is, I know what it would be *like* to give you the moon, though I cannot *in fact* do it. A logically necessary first cause, however, is not impossible in the way that giving you the moon is impossible; no, it is *logically* impossible. "Logically necessary being" is a self-contradictory expression like "round square." It is not any good saying that we would only be intellectually satisfied with a logically necessary cause, that nothing else would do. We can easily have an absurd wish. We should all like to be able to eat our cake and have it, but that does not alter the fact that our wish is an absurd and self-contradictory one. We reject the cosmological argument, then, because it rests on a thorough absurdity.

Having reached this conclusion I should like to make one or two remarks about the necessity of God. First of all, I think that it is undeniable that if worship is to be what religion takes it to be, then God must be a necessary being in some sense or other of "necessary." He must not be just one of the things in the world, however big. To concede that he was just one of the things in the world, even a big one, would reduce religion to something near idolatry. All I wish to point out is that God can not be a *logically* necessary being, for the very supposition that he is is self-contradictory. (Hence, of course, to say that God is not logically necessary is not to place any limitations on him. It is not a limitation on your walking ability that you cannot go out of the room and not go out. To say that someone cannot do something self-contradictory is not to say that he is in any way impotent, it is to say that the sentence "he did such and such and did not do it" is not a possible description of anything.) Theological necessity cannot be logical necessity. In the second place, I think I can see roughly what sort of necessity theological necessity might be. Let me give an analogy from physics. It is not a *logical* necessity that the velocity of light in a vacuum should be constant. It would, however, upset physical theory considerably if we denied it. Similarly it is not a logical necessity that God exists. But it would clearly upset the structure of our religious attitudes in the most violent way if we denied it or even entertained the possibility of its falsehood. So if we say that it is a *physical* necessity that the velocity of light *in vacuo* should be constant— deny it and prevailing physical theory would have to be scrapped or at any rate drastically modified—similarly we can say that it is a *religious* necessity that God exists. That is, we believe in the necessity of God's existence because we are Christians; we are not Christians because we believe in the necessity of God's existence. There are no short cuts to God. I draw your attention to the language of religion itself, where we talk of *conversion*, not of *proof*. In my opinion religion can stand on its own feet, but to found it on a metaphysical argument *a priori* is to found it on absurdity born of ignorance of the logic of our language. I am reminded of what was said about the Boyle lectures in the eighteenth century: that no one doubted that God existed until the Boyle lecturers started to prove it.

Perhaps now is the time to say why I suggested at the beginning of the lecture that "Does God exist?" is not a proper question. Once again I make use of an analogy from science. "Do electrons exist?" (asked just like that) is not a proper question. In order to acquire the concept of an electron we must find out about experiments with cathode-ray tubes, the Wilson cloud chamber, about spectra and so on. We then find the concept of the electron a useful one, one which plays a part in a mass of physical theory. When we reach this stage the question "Do electrons exist?" no longer arises. Before we reached this stage the question "Do electrons exist?" had no clear meaning. Similarly, I suggest, the question "Does God exist?" has no clear meaning for the unconverted. But for the converted the question no longer arises. The word "God" gets its meaning from the part it plays in religious speech and literature, and in religious speech and literature the question of existence does not arise. A theological professor at Glasgow once said to me: "Religion is 'O God, if you exist, save my soul if it exists!' " This of course was a joke. It clearly is just *not* what religion is. So within religion the question "Does God exist?" does not arise, any more than the question "Do electrons exist?" arises within physics. Outside religion the question "Does God exist?" has as little meaning as the question "Do electrons exist?" as asked by the scientifically ignorant. Thus I suggest that it is possible to hold that the question "Does God exist?" is not a proper question without necessarily also holding that religion and theology are nonsensical.

The cosmological argument, we saw, failed because it made use of the absurd conception of a *logically* necessary being. We now pass to the third argument which I propose to consider. This is the *Teleological Argument.* It is also called "the Argument from Design." It would be better called the argument *to* design, as Kemp Smith does call it, for clearly that the universe has been designed by a great architect is to assume a great part of the conclusion to be proved. Or we could call it "the argument from apparent design." The argument is very fully discussed in Hume's *Dialogues concerning Natural Religion,* to which I should like to draw your attention. In these dialogues the argument is presented as follows: "Look round the world: Contemplate the whole and every part of it: You will find it to be nothing but one great machine, subdivided into an infinite number of lesser machines. . . . The curious adapting of means to ends, throughout all nature, resembles exactly, though it much exceeds, the productions of human contrivance. . . . Since therefore the effects resemble each other, we are led to infer, by all the rules of analogy, that the causes also resemble; and that the Author of nature is somewhat similar to the mind of man; though possessed of much larger faculties, proportioned to the grandeur of the work which he has executed."

This argument may at once be criticized in two ways: (1) We may question whether the analogy between the universe and artificial things like houses, ships, furniture, and machines (which admittedly are designed) is very close. Now in any ordinary sense of language, it is true to say that plants and animals have *not* been designed. If we press the analogy of the universe to a plant, instead of to a machine, we get to a very different conclusion. And why should the one analogy be regarded as any better or worse than the other? (2) Even if the analogy were close, it would only go to suggest that the universe was designed by a *very great* (not infinite) architect, and note, an *architect*, not a *creator*. For if we take the analogy seriously we must notice that we do not create the materials from which we make houses, machines and so on, but only *arrange* the materials.

This, in bare outline, is the general objection to the argument from design, and will apply to any form of it. In the form in which the argument was put forward by such theologians as Paley, the argument is, of course, still more open to objection. For Paley laid special stress on such things as the eye of an animal, which he thought must have been contrived by a wise Creator for the special benefit of the animal. It seemed to him inconceivable how otherwise such a complex organ, so well suited to the needs of the animal, should have arisen. Or listen to Henry More: "For why have we three joints in our legs and arms, as also in our fingers, but that it was much better than having two or four? And why are our fore-teeth sharp like chisels to cut, but our inward teeth broad to grind, [instead of] the fore-teeth broad and the other sharp? But we might have made a hard shift to have lived through in that worser condition. Again, why are the teeth so luckily placed, or rather, why are there not teeth in other bones as well as in the jaw-bones? For they might have been as capable as these. But the reason is, nothing is done foolishly or in vain; that is, there is a divine Providence that orders all things." This type of argument has lost its persuasiveness, for the theory of Evolution explains why our teeth are so luckily placed in our jaw-bones, why we have the most convenient number of joints in our fingers, and so on. Species which did not possess advantageous features would not survive in competition with those which did.

The sort of argument Paley and Henry More used is thus quite unconvincing. Let us return to the broader conception, that of the universe as a whole, which seems to show the mark of a benevolent and intelligent Designer. Bacon expressed this belief forcibly: "I had rather beleave all the Fables in the Legend and the Talmud and the Alcoran than that this Universal Frame is without a Minde." So, in some moods, does the universe strike us. But sometimes, when we are in other moods, we see it very differently. To quote Hume's dialogues again: "Look around this Universe. What an immense profusion of beings, animated and organized, sensible and active! You admire this prodigious variety and fecundity. But inspect a little more narrowly these living existences, the only beings worth regarding. How hostile and destructive to each other! How insufficient all of them for their own happiness! . . . The whole presents nothing but the idea of a blind Nature, impregnated by a great vivifying principle, and pouring forth from her lap, without discernment or parental care, her maimed and abortive children!" There is indeed a great deal of suffering, some part of which is no doubt attributable to the moral choices of men, and to save us from which would conflict with what many people would regard as the greater good of moral freedom, but there is still an immense residue of apparently needless suffering, that is, needless in the sense that it could be prevented by an omnipotent being. The difficulty is that of reconciling the presence of evil and suffering with the assertion that God is both omnipotent and benevolent. If we *already* believe in an omnipotent and benevolent God, then some attempt may be made to solve the problem of evil by arguing that the values in the world form a sort of organic unity, and that making any *part* of the world better would perhaps nevertheless reduce the value of the whole. Paradoxical though this thesis may appear at first sight, it is perhaps not theoretically absurd. If, however, evil presents a *difficulty* to the believing mind, it presents an *insuperable* difficulty to one who wishes to argue rationally from the world as we find it to the existence of an omnipotent and benevolent God. As Hume puts it: "Is the world considered in general, and as it appears to us in this life, different from what a man . . . would *beforehand* expect from a very powerful, wise and benevolent Deity? It must be a strange prejudice to assert the contrary. And from thence I conclude, that, however consistent the world may be, allowing certain suppositions and conjectures, with the idea of such a Deity, it can never afford us an inference concerning his existence."

The teleological argument is thus extremely shaky, and in any case, even if it were sound, it would only go to prove the existence of a very great architect, not of an omnipotent and benevolent Creator.

Nevertheless, the argument has a fascination for us that reason can not easily dispel. Hume, in his twelfth dialogue, and after pulling the argument from design to pieces in the previous eleven dialogues, nevertheless speaks as follows: "A purpose, an intention, a design strikes everywhere the most careless, the most stupid thinker; and no man can be so hardened in absurd systems as at all times to reject it . . . all the sciences almost lead us insensibly to acknowledge a first Author." Similarly Kant, before going on to exhibit the fallaciousness of the argument, nevertheless says of it: "This proof always deserves to be mentioned with respect. It is the oldest, the clearest and the most accordant with the common reason of mankind. It enlivens the study of nature, just as it itself derives its existence and gains ever new vigour from that source. It suggests ends and purposes, where our observation would not have detected them by itself, and extends our knowledge of nature by means of the guiding concept of a special unity, the principle of which is outside nature. This knowledge . . . so strengthens the belief in a supreme Author of nature that the belief acquires the force of an irresistible conviction." It is somewhat of a paradox that an invalid argument should command so much respect even from those who have demonstrated its invalidity. The solution of the paradox is perhaps somewhat as follows:[5] The argument from

[5] See also N. Kemp Smith's Henrietta Hertz Lecture, "Is Divine Existence Credible?," *Proceedings of the British Academy*, 1931.

design is no good as an argument. But in those who have the seeds of a genuinely religious attitude already within them the facts to which the argument from design draws attention, facts showing the grandeur and majesty of the universe, facts that are evident to anyone who looks upwards on a starry night, and which are enormously multiplied for us by the advance of theoretical science, these facts have a powerful effect. But they only have this effect on the already religious mind, on the mind which has the capability of feeling the religious type of awe. That is, the argument from design is in reality no argument, or if it is regarded as an argument it is feeble, but it is a potent instrument in heightening religious emotions.

Something similar might even be said of the cosmological argument. As an argument it cannot pass muster at all; indeed it is completely absurd, as employing the notion of a logically necessary being. Nevertheless it does appeal to something deep seated in our natures. It takes its stand on the fact that the existence of you or me or this table is not logically necessary. Logic tells us that this fact is not a fact at all, but is a truism, like the "fact" that a circle is not a square. Again, the cosmological argument tries to base the existence of you or me or this table on the existence of a logically necessary being, and hence commits a rank absurdity, the notion of a logically necessary being being self-contradictory. So the only rational thing to say if someone asks "Why does this table exist?" is some such thing as that such and such a carpenter made it. We can go back and back in such a series, but we must not entertain the absurd idea of getting back to something logically necessary. However, now let us ask, "Why should anything exist at all?" Logic seems to tell us that the only answer which is not absurd is to say, "Why shouldn't it?" Nevertheless, though I know how any answer on the lines of the cosmological argument can be pulled to pieces by a correct logic, I still feel I want to go on asking the question. Indeed, though logic has taught me to look at such a question with the gravest suspicion, my mind often seems to reel under the immense significance it seems to have for me. That anything should exist at all does seem to me a matter for the deepest awe. But whether other people feel this sort of awe, and whether they or I ought to is another question. I think we ought to. If so, the question arises: If "Why should anything exist at all?" cannot be interpreted after the manner of the cosmological argument, that is, as an absurd request for the nonsensical postulation of a logically necessary being, what sort of question is it? What sort of question is this question "Why should anything exist at all?" All I can say is, that I do not yet know.

The Problem of Evil

David Hume (1711–1776) was a British philosopher and historian, and one of the principal developers of the empiricist tradition in modern philosophy. His main philosophical works include *A Treatise of Human Nature, Inquiry Concerning Human Understanding,* and *Dialogues Concerning Natural Religion.*

And is it possible, *Cleanthes,* said *Philo,* that after all these reflections, and infinitely more, which might be suggested, you can still persevere in your Anthropomorphism, and assert the moral attributes of the Deity, his justice, benevolence, mercy, and rectitude, to be of the same nature with these virtues in human creatures? His power we allow infinite: whatever he wills is executed: but neither man nor any other animal is happy: therefore he does not will their happiness. His wisdom is infinite: he is never mistaken in choosing the means to any end: but the course of nature tends not to human or animal felicity: therefore it is not established for that purpose. Through the whole compass of human knowledge, there are no inferences more certain and infallible than these. In what respect, then, do his benevolence and mercy resemble the benevolence and mercy of men?

* From David Hume, *Dialogues Concerning Natural Religion.*

Epicurus's old questions are yet unanswered.

Is he willing to prevent evil, but not able? then is he impotent. Is he able, but not willing? then is he malevolent. Is he both able and willing? whence then is evil?

You ascribe, *Cleanthes,* (and I believe justly) a purpose and intention to Nature. But what, I beseech you, is the object of that curious artifice and machinery, which she has displayed in all animals? The preservation alone of individuals and propagation of the species. It seems enough for her purpose, if such a rank be barely upheld in the universe, without any care or concern for the happiness of the members that compose it. No resource for this purpose: no machinery, in order merely to give pleasure or ease: no fund of pure joy and contentment: no indulgence without some want or necessity accompanying it. At least, the few phenomena of this nature are overbalanced by opposite phenomena of still greater importance.

Our sense of music, harmony, and indeed beauty of all kinds, gives satisfaction, without being absolutely necessary to the preservation and propagation of the species. But what racking pains, on the other hand, arise from gouts, gravels, megrims, toothaches, rheumatisms; where the injury to the animal-machinery is either small or incurable? Mirth, laughter, play, frolic, seem gratuitous satisfactions, which have no farther tendency: spleen, melancholy, discontent, superstition, are pains of the same nature. How then does the divine benevolence display itself, in the sense of you Anthropomorphites? None but we Mystics, as you were pleased to call us, can account for this strange mixture of phenomena, by deriving it from attributes, infinitely perfect, but incomprehensible.

And have you at last, said *Cleanthes* smiling, betrayed your intentions, *Philo?* Your long agreement with *Demea* did indeed a little surprise me; but I find you were all the while erecting a concealed battery against me. And I must confess, that you have now fallen upon a subject, worthy of your noble spirit of opposition and controversy. If you can make out the present point, and prove mankind to be unhappy or corrupted, there is an end at once of all religion. For to what purpose establish the natural attributes of the Deity, while the moral are still doubtful and uncertain?

You take umbrage very easily, replied *Demea,* at opinions the most innocent, and the most generally received even amongst the religious and devout themselves: and nothing can be more surprising than to find a topic like this, concerning the wickedness and misery of man, charged with no less than Atheism and profaneness. Have not all pious divines and preachers, who have indulged their rhetoric on so fertile a subject; have they not easily, I say, given a solution of any difficulties, which may attend it? This world is but a point in comparison of the universe; this life but a moment in comparison of eternity. The present evil phenomena, therefore, are rectified in other regions, and in some future period of existence. And the eyes of men, being then opened to larger views of things, see the whole connection of general laws; and trace, with adoration, the benevolence and rectitude of the Deity, through all the mazes and intricacies of his providence.

No! replied *Cleanthes,* No! These arbitrary suppositions can never be admitted, contrary to matter of fact, visible and uncontroverted. Whence can any cause be known but from its known effects? Whence can any hypothesis be proved but from the apparent phenomena? To establish one hypothesis upon another, is building entirely in the air; and the utmost we ever attain, by these conjectures and fictions, is to ascertain the bare possibility of our opinion; but never can we, upon such terms, establish its reality.

The only method of supporting divine benevolence (and it is what I willingly embrace) is to deny absolutely the misery and wickedness of man. Your representations are exaggerated: Your melancholy views mostly fictitious: Your inferences contrary to fact and experience. Health is more common than sickness: Pleasure than pain: Happiness than misery. And for one vexation, which we meet with, we attain, upon computation, a hundred enjoyments.

Admitting your position, replied *Philo,* which yet is extremely doubtful, you must, at the same time, allow, that, if pain be less frequent than pleasure, it is infinitely more violent and durable. One hour of it is often able to outweigh a day, a week, a month of our common insipid enjoyments: And how many days, weeks, and months are passed by several in the most acute torments? Pleasure, scarcely in one instance, is ever able to reach ecstacy and rapture:

And in no one instance can it continue for any time at its highest pitch and altitude. The spirits evaporate; the nerves relax; the fabric is disordered; and the enjoyment quickly degenerates into fatigue and uneasiness. But pain often, good God, how often! rises to torture and agony; and the longer it continues, it becomes still more genuine agony and torture. Patience is exhausted; courage languishes; melancholy seizes us; and nothing terminates our misery but the removal of its cause, or another event, which is the sole cure of all evil, but which, from our natural folly, we regard with still greater horror and consternation.

But not to insist upon these topics, continued *Philo*, though most obvious, certain, and important; I must use the freedom to admonish you, *Cleanthes*, that you have put this controversy upon a most dangerous issue, and are unawares introducing a total Scepticism, into the most essential articles of natural and revealed theology. What! no method of fixing a just foundation for religion, unless we allow the happiness of human life, and maintain a continued existence even in this world, with all our present pains, infirmities, vexations, and follies, to be eligible and desirable! But this is contrary to every one's feeling and experience: It is contrary to an authority so established as nothing can subvert: No decisive proofs can ever be produced against this authority; nor is it possible for you to compute, estimate, and compare all the pains and all the pleasures in the lives of all men and of all animals: And thus by your resting the whole system of religion on a point, which, from its very nature, must for ever be uncertain, you tacitly confess, that that system is equally uncertain.

But allowing you, what never will be believed; at least, what you never possibly can prove, that animal, or at least, human happiness, in this life, exceeds its misery; you have yet done nothing: For this is not, by any means, what we expect from infinite power, infinite wisdom, and infinite goodness. Why is there any misery at all in the world? Not by chance surely. From some cause then. Is it from the intention of the Deity? But he is perfectly benevolent. Is it contrary to his intention? But he is almighty. Nothing can shake the solidity of this reasoning, so short, so clear, so decisive; except we assert, that these subjects exceed all human capacity, and that our common measures of truth and falsehood are not applicable to them; a topic, which I have all along insisted on, but which you have, from the beginning, rejected with scorn and indignation.

But I will be contented to retire still from this intrenchment: For I deny that you can ever force me in it: I will allow, that pain or misery in man is *compatible* with infinite power and goodness in the Deity, even in your sense of these attributes: What are you advanced by all these concessions? A mere possible compatibility is not sufficient. You must *prove* these pure, unmixed, and uncontrollable attributes from the present mixed and confused phenomena, and from these alone. A hopeful undertaking! Were the phenomena ever so pure and unmixed, yet being finite, they would be insufficient for that purpose. How much more, where they are also so jarring and discordant!

Here, *Cleanthes,* I find myself at ease in my argument. Here I triumph. Formerly, when we argued concerning the natural attributes of intelligence and design, I needed all my sceptical and metaphysical subtilty to elude your grasp. In many views of the universe, and of its parts, particularly the latter, the beauty and fitness of final causes strike us with such irresistible force, that all objections appear (what I believe they really are) mere cavils and sophisms; nor can we then imagine how it was ever possible for us to repose any weight on them. But there is no view of human life or of the condition of mankind, from which, without the greatest violence, we can infer the moral attributes, or learn that infinite benevolence, conjoined with infinite power and infinite wisdom, which we must discover by the eyes of faith alone. It is your turn now to tug the labouring oar, and to support your philosophical subtilties against the dictates of plain reason and experience.

I scruple not to allow, said *Cleanthes,* that I have been apt to suspect the frequent repetition of the word, *infinite,* which we meet with in all theological writers, to savour more of panegyric than of philosophy, and that any purposes of reasoning, and even of religion, would be better served, were we to rest contented with more accurate and more moderate expressions. The terms, *admirable, excellent, superlatively great, wise,* and *holy;* these sufficiently fill the imaginations of men; and any thing beyond, besides that it leads into absurdities, has no influence on your affections or sentiments. Thus, in the present subject, if we abandon all human analogy, as seems your intention, *Demea,* I am afraid we abandon all religion, and retain no conception of the great object of our adoration. If we preserve human analogy, we must for ever find it impossible to reconcile any mixture of evil in the universe with infinite attributes; much less can we ever prove the latter from the former. But supposing the Author of Nature to be finitely perfect, though far exceeding mankind; a satisfactory account may then be given of natural and moral evil, and every untoward phenomenon be explained and adjusted. A less evil may then be chosen, in order to avoid a greater; Inconveniences be submitted to, in order to reach a desirable end: And in a word, benevolence, regulated by wisdom, and limited by necessity, may produce just such a world as the present. You, *Philo,* who are so prompt at starting views, and reflections, and analogies, I would gladly hear, at length, without interruption, your opinion of this new theory; and if it deserve our attention, we may afterwards, at more leisure, reduce it into form.

My sentiments, replied *Philo,* are not worth being made a mystery of; and therefore, without any ceremony, I shall deliver what occurs to me with regard to the present subject. It must, I think, be allowed, that, if a very limited intelligence, whom we shall suppose utterly unacquainted with the universe, were assured, that it were the production of a very good, wise, and powerful being, however finite, he would, from his conjectures, form *beforehand* a different notion of it from what we find it to be by experience; nor would he ever imagine, merely from these attributes of the cause, of which he is informed, that the effect could be so full of vice and misery and disorder, as it appears in this life. Supposing now, that this person were brought into the world, still assured, that it was the workmanship of such a sublime and benevolent Being; he might, perhaps, be surprised at the disappointment; but would never retract his former belief, if founded on any very solid argument; since such a limited intelligence must be sensible of his own blindness and ignorance, and must allow, that there may be many solutions of those phenomena, which will for ever escape his comprehension. But supposing, which is the real case with regard to man, that this creature is not antecedently convinced of a supreme intelligence, benevolent, and powerful, but is left to gather such a belief from the appearances of things; this entirely alters the case, nor will he ever find any reason for such a conclusion. He may be fully convinced of the narrow limits of his understanding; but this will not help him in forming an inference concerning the goodness of superior powers, since he must form that inference from what he knows, not from what he is ignorant of. The more you exaggerate his weakness and ignorance, the more diffident you render him, and give him the greater suspicion, that such subjects are beyond the reach of his faculties. You are obliged, therefore, to reason with him merely from the known phenomena, and to drop every arbitrary supposition or conjecture.

Did I show you a house or palace, where there was not one apartment convenient or agreeable; where the windows, doors, fires, passages, stairs, and the whole economy of the building were the source of noise, confusion, fatigue, darkness, and the extremes of heat and cold; you would certainly blame the contrivance, without any farther examination. The architect would in vain display his subtilty, and prove to you, that if this door or that window were altered, greater ills would ensue. What he says, may be strictly true: The alteration of one particular, while the other parts of the building remain, may only augment the inconveniences. But still you would assert in general, that, if the architect had had skill and good intentions, he might have formed such a plan of the whole, and might have adjusted the parts in such a manner, as would have remedied all or most of these inconveniences. His ignorance, or even your own ignorance of such a plan, will never convince you of the impossibility of it. If you find many inconveniences and deformities in the building, you will always, without entering into any detail, condemn the architect.

In short, I repeat the question: Is the world considered in general, and as it appears to us in this life, different from what a man or such a limited Being would, *beforehand*, expect from a very powerful, wise, and benevolent Deity? It must be strange prejudice to assert the contrary. And from thence I conclude, that, however consistent the world may be, allowing certain suppositions and conjectures, with the idea of such a Deity, it can never afford us an inference concerning his existence. The consistence is not absolutely denied, only the inference. Conjectures, especially where infinity is excluded from the Divine attributes, may perhaps be sufficient to prove a consistence; but can never be foundations for any inference.

There seem to be *four* circumstances, on which depend all, or the greatest parts of the ills, that molest sensible creatures; and it is not impossible but all these circumstances may be necessary and unavoidable. We know so little beyond common life, or even of common life, that, with regard to the economy of a universe, there is no conjecture, however wild, which may not be just; nor any one, however plausible, which may not be erroneous. All that belongs to human understanding, in this deep ignorance and obscurity, is to be sceptical, or at least cautious; and not to admit of any hypothesis, whatever; much less, of any which is supported by no appearance of probability. Now this I assert to be the case with regard to all the causes of evil, and the circumstances, on which it depends. None of them appear to human reason, in the least degree, necessary or unavoidable; nor can we suppose them such, without the utmost licence of imagination.

The *first circumstance* which introduces evil, is that contrivance or economy of the animal creation, by which pains, as well as pleasures, are employed to excite all creatures to action, and make them vigilant in the great work of self-preservation. Now pleasure alone, in its various degrees, seems to human understanding sufficient for this purpose. All animals might be constantly in a state of enjoyment; but when urged by any of the necessities of nature, such as thirst, hunger, weariness; instead of pain, they might feel a diminution of pleasure, by which they might be prompted to seek that object, which is necessary to their subsistence. Men pursue pleasure as eagerly as they avoid pain; at least, might have been so constituted. It seems, therefore, plainly possible to carry on the business of life without any pain. Why then is any animal ever rendered susceptible of such a sensation? If animals can be free from it an hour, they might enjoy a perpetual exemption from it; and it required as particular a contrivance of their organs to produce that feeling, as to endow them with sight, hearing, or any of the senses. Shall we conjecture, that such a contrivance was necessary, without any appearance of reason? and shall we build on that conjecture as on the most certain truth?

But a capacity of pain would not alone produce pain, were it not for the *second* circumstance, namely, the conducting of the world by general laws; and this seems nowise necessary to a very perfect being. It is true; if every thing were conducted by particular volitions, the course of nature would be perpetually broken, and no man could employ his reason in the conduct of life. But might not other particular volitions remedy this inconvenience? In short, might not the Deity exterminate all ill, wherever it were to be found; and produce all good, without any preparation or long progress of causes and effects?

Besides, we must consider, that, according to the present economy of the world, the course of Nature, though supposed exactly regular, yet to us appears not so, and many events are uncertain, and many disappoint our expectations. Health and sickness, calm and tempest, with an infinite number of other accidents, whose causes are unknown and variable, have a great influence both on the fortunes of particular persons and on the prosperity of public societies: and indeed all human life, in a manner, depends on such accidents. A being, therefore, who knows the secret springs of the universe, might easily, by particular volitions, turn all these accidents to the good of mankind, and render the whole world happy, without discovering himself in any operation. A fleet, whose purposes were salutary to society, might always meet with a fair wind: Good princes enjoy sound health and long life: Persons, born to power and authority, be framed with good tempers and virtuous dispositions. A few such events as these, regularly and wisely conducted, would change the face of the world; and yet would no more seem to disturb the course of Nature or confound human conduct, than the present economy of things, where the causes are secret, and variable, and compounded. Some small touches, given to *Caligula's* brain in his infancy, might have converted him into a *Trajan:* one wave, a little higher than the rest, by burying *Cæsar* and his fortune in the bottom of the ocean, might have restored liberty to a considerable part of mankind. There may, for aught we know, be good reasons, why Providence interposes not in this manner; but they are unknown to us: and though the mere supposition, that such reasons exist, may be sufficient to *save* the conclusion concerning the divine attributes, yet surely it can never be sufficient to *establish* that conclusion.

If every thing in the universe be conducted by general laws, and if animals be rendered susceptible of pain, it scarcely seems possible but some ill must arise in the various shocks of matter, and the various concurrence and opposition of general laws: But this ill would be very rare, were it not for the *third* circumstance, which I proposed to mention, namely, the great frugality with which all powers and faculties are distributed to every particular being. So well adjusted are the organs and capacities of all animals, and so well fitted to their preservation, that, as far as history or tradition reaches, there appears not to be any single species, which has yet been extinguished in the universe. Every animal has the requisite endowments; but these endowments are bestowed with so scrupulous an economy, that any considerable diminution must entirely destroy the creature. Wherever one power is increased, there is a proportional abatement in the others. Animals, which excel in swiftness, are commonly defective in force. Those, which possess both, are either imperfect in some of their senses, or are oppressed with the most craving wants. The human species, whose chief excellency is reason and sagacity, is of all others the most necessitous, and the most deficient in bodily advantages; without clothes, without arms, without food, without lodging, without any convenience of life, except what they owe to their own skill and industry. In short, Nature seems to have formed an exact calculation of the necessities of her creatures; and like a *rigid master,* has afforded them little more powers or endowments, than what are strictly sufficient to supply those necessities. An *indulgent parent* would have bestowed a large stock, in order to guard against accidents, and secure the happiness and welfare of the creature, in the most unfortunate concurrence of circumstances. Every course of life would not have been so surrounded with precipices, that the least departure from the true path, by mistake or necessity, must involve us in misery and ruin. Some reserve, some fund would have been provided to ensure happiness; nor would the powers and the necessities have been adjusted with so rigid an economy. The author of Nature is inconceivably powerful: his force is supposed great, if not altogether inexhaustible: nor is there any reason, as far as we can judge, to make him observe this strict frugality in his dealings with his creatures. It would have been better, were his power extremely limited, to have created fewer animals, and to have endowed these with more faculties for their happiness and preservation. A builder is never esteemed prudent, who undertakes a plan, beyond what his stock will enable him to finish.

In order to cure most of the ills of human life, I require not that man should have the wings of the eagle, the swiftness of the stag, the force of the ox, the arms of the lion, the scales of the crocodile or rhinoceros; much less do I demand the sagacity of an angel or cherubin. I am contented to take an increase in one single power or faculty of his soul. Let him be endowed with a greater propensity to industry and labour; a more vigorous spring and activity of mind; a more constant bent to business and application. Let the whole species possess naturally an equal diligence with that which many individuals are able to attain by habit and reflection; and the most beneficial consequences, without any alloy of ill, is the immediate and necessary result of this endowment. Almost all the moral, as well as natural evils of human life arise from idleness; and were our species, by the original constitution of their frame, exempt from this vice or infirmity, the perfect cultivation of land, the improvement of arts and manufactures, the exact execution of every office and duty, immediately follow; and men at once may fully reach that state of society, which is so imperfectly attained by the best-regulated government. But as industry is a power, and the most valuable of any, Nature seems determined, suitably to her usual maxims, to bestow it on men with a very sparing hand; and rather to punish him severely for his deficiency in it, than to reward him for his attainments. She has so contrived his frame, that nothing but the most violent necessity can oblige him to labour; and she employs all his other wants to overcome, at least in part, the want of diligence, and to endow him with some share of a faculty, of which she has thought fit naturally to bereave him. Here our demands may be allowed very humble, and therefore the more reasonable. If we required the endowments of superior penetration and judgment, of a more delicate taste of beauty, of a nicer sensibility to benevolence and friendship; we might be told, that we impiously pretend to break the order of Nature, that we want to exalt ourselves into a higher rank of being, that the presents which we require, not being suitable to our state and condition, would only be pernicious to us. But it is hard; I dare to repeat it, it is hard, that being placed in a world so full of wants and necessities; where almost every being and element is either our foe or refuses us their assistance, . . . we should also have our own temper to struggle with, and should be deprived of that faculty, which can alone fence against these multiplied evils.

The *fourth* circumstance, whence arises the misery and ill of the universe, is the inaccurate workmanship of all the springs and principles of the great machine of nature. It must be acknowledged, that there are few parts of the universe, which seem not to serve some purpose, and whose removal would not produce a visible defect and disorder in the whole. The parts hang all together; nor can one be touched without affecting the rest in a greater or less degree. But at the same time, it must be observed, that none of these parts or principles, however useful, are so accurately adjusted, as to keep precisely within those bounds, in which their utility consists; but they are, all of them, apt, on every occasion, to run into the one extreme or the other. One would imagine, that this grand production had not received the last hand of the maker; so little finished is every part, and so coarse are the strokes, with which it is executed. Thus, the winds are requisite to convey the vapours along the surface of the globe, and to assist men in navigation: but how oft, rising up to tempests and hurricanes, do they become pernicious? Rains are necessary to nourish all the plants and animals of the earth: but how often are they defective? how often excessive? Heat is requisite to all life and vegetation; but is not always found in the due proportion. On the mixture and secretion of the humours and juices of the body depend the health and prosperity of the animal: but the parts perform not regularly their proper function. What more useful than all the passions of the mind, ambition, vanity, love, anger? But how oft do they break their bounds, and cause the greatest convulsions in society? There is nothing so advantageous in the universe, but what frequently becomes pernicious, by its excess or defect; nor has Nature guarded, with the requisite accuracy, against all disorder or confusion. The irregularity is never, perhaps, so great as to destroy any species; but is often sufficient to involve the individuals in ruin and misery.

On the concurrence, then, of these *four* circumstances does all, or the greatest part of natural evil depend. Were all living creatures incapable of pain, or were the world administered by particular volitions, evil never could have found access into the universe: and were animals endowed with a large stock of powers and faculties, beyond what strict necessity requires; or were the several springs and principles of the universe so accurately framed as to preserve always the just temperament and medium; there must have been little ill in comparison of what we feel at present. What then shall we pronounce on this occasion? Shall we say, that these circumstances are not necessary, and that they might easily have been altered in the contrivance of the universe? This decision seems too presumptuous for creatures, so blind and ignorant. Let us be more modest in our conclusions. Let us allow, that, if the goodness of the Deity (I mean a goodness like the human) could be established on any tolerable reasons *a priori*, these phenomena, however untoward, would not be sufficient to subvert that principle; but might easily, in some unknown manner, be reconcilable to it. But let us still assert, that as this goodness is not antecedently established, but must be inferred from the phenomena, there can be no grounds for such an inference, while there are so many ills in the universe, and while these ills might so easily have been remedied, as far as human understanding can be allowed to judge on such a subject. I am Sceptic enough to allow, that the bad appearances, notwithstanding all my reasonings, may be compatible with such attributes as you suppose: But surely they can never prove these attributes. Such a conclusion cannot result from Scepticism; but must arise from the phenomena, and from our confidence in the reasonings, which we deduce from these phenomena.

Look round this universe. What an immense profusion of beings, animated and organized, sensible and active! You admire this prodigious variety and fecundity. But inspect a little more narrowly these living existences, the only beings worth regarding. How hostile and destructive to each other! How insufficient all of them for their own happiness! How contemptible or odious to the spectator! The whole presents nothing but the idea of a blind Nature, impregnated by a great vivifying principle, and pouring forth from her lap, without discernment or parental care, her maimed and abortive children!

Here the *Manichæan* system occurs as a proper hypothesis to solve the difficulty: and no doubt, in some respects, it is very specious, and has more probability than the common hypothesis, by giving a plausible account of the strange mixture of good and ill, which appears in life. But if we consider, on the other hand, the perfect uniformity and agreement of the parts of the universe, we shall not discover in it any marks of the combat of a malevolent with a benevolent being. There is indeed an opposition of pains and pleasures in the feelings of sensible creatures: but are not all the operations of Nature carried on by an opposition of principles, of hot and cold, moist and dry, light and heavy? The true conclusion is, that the original source of all things is entirely indifferent to all these principles, and has no more regard to good above ill than to heat above cold, or to drought above moisture, or to light above heavy.

There may *four* hypotheses be framed concerning the first causes of the universe: *that* they are endowed with perfect goodness, *that* they have perfect malice, *that* they are opposite and have both goodness and malice, *that* they have neither goodness nor malice. Mixed phenomena can never prove the two former unmixed principles. And the uniformity and steadiness of general laws seem to oppose the third. The fourth, therefore, seems by far the most probable.

What I have said concerning natural evil will apply to moral, with little or no variation; and we have no more reason to infer, that the rectitude of the Supreme Being resembles human rectitude than that his benevolence resembles the human. Nay, it will be thought, that we have still greater cause to exclude from him moral sentiments, such as we feel them; since evil, in the opinion of many, is much more predominant above moral good than natural evil above natural good.

But even though this should not be allowed, and though the virtue, which is in mankind, should be acknowledged much superior to the vice; yet so long as there is any vice at all in the universe, it will very much puzzle you Anthropomorphites, how to account for it. You must assign a cause for it, without having recourse to the first cause. But as every effect must have a cause, and that cause another; you must either carry on the progression *in infinitum*, or rest on that original principle, who is the ultimate cause of all things . . . .

JOHN BAILLIE

The Experience of God

John Baillie (1886–1960) was a British theologian and philosopher. Some of his published works are *And the Life Everlasting, Our Knowledge of God, Invitation to Pilgrimage, The Idea of Revelation in Recent Thought,* and *The Sense of the Presence of God.*

The witness of all true religion is that there is no reality which more directly confronts us than the reality of God. No other reality is nearer to us than He. The realities of sense are more obvious, but His is the more intimate, touching us as it does so much nearer to the core of our being. God's approach to us in Christ is the closest approach that is ever made to the inmost citadel of our souls—

> The hold that falls not when the town is got,
> The heart's heart, whose immurèd plot
> Hath keys yourself keep not! [1]

"Behold, I stand at the door and knock," says Christ; and though many knockings are more obtrusive, none is so patient or in the

---

* Reprinted with the permission of Charles Scribner's Sons from *Our Knowledge of God,* pp. 155–159, 178–189, by John Baillie. Copyright © 1959 John Baillie.

[1] Francis Thompson, *A Fallen Yew.*

last resort so ineluctable. God alone is omnipresent. His is the only claim that is always with us and never lets us go. "Whither shall I go from thy spirit? or whither shall I flee from thy presence? If I ascend up into heaven, thou art there: if I make my bed in Sheol, behold, thou art there. If I take the wings of the morning, and dwell in the uttermost parts of the sea; Even there shall thy hand lead me, and thy right hand shall hold me. If I say, Surely the darkness shall cover me; even the night shall be light about me. Yea, the darkness hideth not from thee, but the night shineth as the day: the darkness and the light are both alike to thee." [2] I am sure that, in proportion as we are honest with ourselves, we shall all have to confess to this haunting Presence. It has been with us from our youth up, and we know that it will be with us to the end. No other challenge that has ever reached us has been so insistent or so imperious. You and I have often tried to evade it; we have done many things in its despite; sometimes, when its demands were most inconvenient, we have tried to pretend that it had no right to be there at all. But in the bottom of our hearts we have never been able to doubt its right. We have always known that there is no other sovereign right but this, and no other "totalitarian" authority. We are surrounded by many glaring realities that occupy the foreground of our consciousness and make all sorts of claims on our attention and allegiance; but we have always known that only one obligation is absolute and one imperative categorical. Moreover, you and I have always known that this claim that was being made upon us was being made upon us for our *good,* and that in yielding to it lay our only true salvation. Even when we most tried to escape from it, we still knew that our deepest weal lay in obedience. We knew that it was sovereign Love that was here constraining us and claiming us for its own; and we knew that in the last resort it was something that was being *offered* us rather than asked of us—and that what was being asked of us was only that we should accept the offer. So when men gazed upon the figure of the Crucified Christ, they were conscious of all the rebuke it held for them, all the condemnation of their sin, all the rigour

[2] *Psalms* cxxxix.

and austerity of its demands; but behind all they knew most certainly that "herein was love." "For God sent not his Son into the world to condemn the world; but that the world through him might be saved." [3]

I have already spoken of the Kantian revolution as that next following upon the Cartesian in the order of modern thought. In Kant's Critical Philosophy there is a most valuable recovery of the fundamental truth upon which I have been dwelling, yet Kant was still too much in bondage to the humanistic tradition, and particularly to the eighteenth-century stratum of that tradition, to let it appear in anything but a sadly curtailed and impoverished form. Kant's great rediscovery was that of the Primacy of the Practical Reason, as he called it. It is not in the realm of sense, he believed, that we are all really in touch with absolute objective reality, and certainly not in the realm of the supersensible objects of scientific and metaphysical speculation, but only in the realm of the practical claim that is made upon our wills by the Good. Ultimate reality meets us, not in the form of an object that invites our speculation, but in the form of a demand that is made upon our obedience. We are confronted not with an absolute object of theoretical knowledge but with an absolute obligation. We reach the Unconditional only in an unconditional imperative that reaches us. There is here, as it seems to me, most precious and deeply Christian insight. But where Kant erred, and where his eighteenth-century education was too much for him, was in his analysis of this experience into mere *respect for a law*. The eighteenth century had its own very remarkable greatness, but it also had its obvious limitations—limitations which could not, in fact, be better exemplified than in this proposal to make *law* at once the primary fact in the universe and the prime object of our *respect*. Something of this respect for law we can still conjure up as we stroll through the well-ordered palace and gardens of Versailles, or again as we wander at will through the equally well-ordered couplets of Alexander Pope's poetry; yet between us and both of these experiences stands that Romantic Revival which, in spite of all its regrettable extrava-

[3] *John* iii, 17.

gances, has taught us a delight in *fera natura* of which we shall
never again be able entirely to rid ourselves. The reduction of the
spiritual life of mankind to the mere respectful acceptance of a
formula was, in fact, the last absurdity of the eighteenth century.
It is no mere formula with which the sons of men have ever found
themselves faced as they approached life's most solemn issues, but
a Reality of an altogether more intimate and personal kind;[4] and
respect or *Achtung* is hardly an adequate name for all the fear and
the holy dread, the love and the passionate self-surrender, with
which they have responded to its presence. We must indeed do
Kant the justice of remembering that he discovered a process of
reasoning which, as he thought, justified him in envisaging this
moral law in a more concrete way as the commandment of a holy
God. In this way something of the true spiritual life of mankind
seems to find its way back into his scheme. Yet the loophole by
which it is allowed to enter is so narrow that little or nothing of
the rich reality of it succeeds in getting through. Kant's religion
remained to the end a mere legalistic moralism *plus* a syllogism that
allowed him to conceive of an eighteenth-century Legislator behind
His eighteenth-century law. "Thus," as—to take only one example—
he himself most cogently concluded, "the purpose of prayer can
only be to induce in us a moral disposition. . . . To wish to converse with God is absurd: we cannot talk to one we cannot intuit;
and as we cannot intuit God, but can only believe in him, we cannot converse with him." [5]

Now it seems to me that it is precisely such a sense of *converse*
with the Living God as Kant thus clearly saw to be excluded by his
own system that lies at the root of all our spiritual life. That life
finds its only beginning in the revelation to our finite minds of One
whose transcendent perfection constitutes upon our lives a claim so
sovereign that the least attempt to deny it awakens in us a sense

---

[4] "For no law, apart from a Lawgiver, is a proper object of reverence. It is
mere brute fact; and every living thing, still more every person exercising intelligent choice, is its superior. The reverence of persons can be appropriately
given only to that which itself is at least personal."—Archbishop William
Temple, *Nature, Man and God*, p. 255. Dr. Temple italicizes the whole passage.
[5] *Lectures on Ethics*, trans. by L. Infield, p. 99.

of sin and shame; and thus is initiated the sequence, ever extending itself as the revelation of the divine nature becomes deeper and fuller, of confession, repentance, forgiveness, reconciliation, and the new life of fellowship. *There is no other spiritual sequence than this.*

. . . .

Yet, though we are more directly and intimately confronted with the presence of God than with any other presence, it does not follow that He is ever present to us *apart* from all other presences. And, in fact, it is the witness of experience that only "in, with and under" other presences is the divine presence ever vouchsafed to us. This aspect of the matter was referred to at the beginning of this chapter, but must now be more fully investigated.

I believe the view to be capable of defence that no one of the four subjects of our knowledge—ourselves, our fellows, the corporeal world, and God—is ever presented to us except in conjunction with all three of the others. Here, however, we need only concern ourselves with the fact that God does not present Himself to us except in conjunction with the presence of our fellows and of the corporeal world.

Taking the second point first, it seems plain that the consciousness of God is never given save in conjunction with the consciousness of things. We do not know God through the world, but we know Him with the world; and in knowing Him with the world, we know Him as its ground. Nature is not an argument for God, but it is a sacrament of Him. Just as in the sacrament of Holy Communion the Real Presence of Christ is given (if the Lutheran phrase may here be used without prejudice) "in, with and under" the bread and wine, so in a wider sense the whole corporeal world may become sacramental to us of the presence of the Triune God. The conception of a sacramental universe thus expresses the truth that lay behind St. Thomas's natural theology, while being free from the errors in which the latter became involved. No writer has done more to clarify our thought on this matter than Baron von Hügel. "Necessity of the Thing-element in Religion" is not only the title of a section in his greatest work,[6] but a constant

---

[6] *The Mystical Element in Religion*, 2nd edition, Vol. II, pp. 372 ff.

theme in all his works. "Spirit," he tells us, "is awakened on occasion of Sense." [7] The knowledge of God, he insists, is not during this life given to us in its isolated purity, but only through "the humiliations of the material order." [8] The knowledge of God which we have on earth is of a kind that we cannot conceive to exist apart from some knowledge of things.

But it is equally certain that all our knowledge of God is given us "in, with and under" our knowledge of one another. This means, first, that the knowledge of God is withholden from those who keep themselves aloof from the *service* of their fellows. It means that "He that loveth not knoweth not God," [9] whereas "if we love one another, God dwelleth in us." [10] And this is indeed a blessed provision by which God makes my knowledge of Himself pass through my brother's need. It means, second, that only when I am in *fellowship* with my fellow men does the knowledge of God come to me individually. It means the necessity of the Church and the rejection of religious individualism. It gives the true sense of the Cyprianic formula, *extra ecclesiam nulla salus.* "For where two or three are gathered together in my name, there am I in the midst of them." [11] Such was the promise; and its fulfilment came when the disciples "were *all* with one accord in one place" and the Spirit "sat upon *each* of them." [12] It means, third, the necessity of history. There is a necessary historical element in all religion, for we know of no religion that is not dependent on tradition; but Christianity is plainly an historical religion in the fullest possible sense. The Christian knowledge of God is not given to any man save in conjunction with the telling of an "old, old story." Therefore it means, lastly, the necessity of Christ, God incarnate in the flesh. "For there is one God, and one mediator between God and men, the man Christ Jesus; who gave himself a ransom for all, to be testified in due

[7] *Essays and Addresses,* 2nd series, p. 246.
[8] See the chapter on "The Natural Order" in M. Nédoncelle's *Baron Friedrich von Hügel.*
[9] *1 John* iv. 8.
[10] *1 John* iv. 12.
[11] *Matthew* xviii. 20.
[12] *Acts* ii. 1–3.

time." [13] The service of others, the fellowship with others, and the historical tradition in which I stand are all media that lead me to the Mediator, and the Mediator leads me to God. And all this mediation is part of God's gracious purpose in refusing to unite me to Himself without at the same time uniting me to my fellow men—in making it impossible for me to obey either of the two great commandments without at the same time obeying the other. This understanding of the relation of faith to history is one which has been greatly clarified for us by Dr. Gogarten and other writers of his school.[14] It is finely summarized by Dr. Brunner: "However inconceivable for us the miracle of the Incarnation may be, yet God lets us in some measure learn why his revelation happens precisely thus and in no other way. It is the wisdom and the goodness of the ruler of the world that he has revealed himself once for all at a particular place, at a particular time. Inasmuch as God, so to speak, deposits his gift of salvation at this one historical place, he compels at the same time all men who wish to share in this gift to betake themselves to this one place, and there to meet each other. . . . It is as if God had used a stratagem by so revealing himself that he can only be found when we find our brother along with him, that in order to find him we must let ourselves be bound to our brother. Only in the bond which unites me to the historical fellowship of my fellow believers—to be more exact, in the fellowship of those who believed before me—is my faith possible. . . . I must, so to speak, submit to becoming myself a member of the fellowship, if I wish to enter into relation with God. God will not bind me to himself on any other terms than these, that he binds me at the same time to my brother." [15]

Clearly, then, the immediacy of God's presence to our souls is a mediated immediacy. But I must now do what I can to resolve the apparent self-contradictoriness of this phrase.

What I must do is to ask myself how the knowledge of God first

[13] *1 Timothy* ii. 5–6.

[14] See especially F. Gogarten, *Ich Glaube an den Dreieinigen Gott: eine Untersuchung über Glauben und Geschichte* (1926); *Glaube und Wirklichkeit* (1928).

[15] *God and Man,* English translation, p. 126 f.

came to me. And here I can only repeat what was said in the open-ing pages of this book: unless my analysis of my memory is alto-gether at fault, the knowledge of God first came to me in the form of an awareness that I was "not my own" but one under authority, one who "owed" something, one who "ought" to be something which he was not. But whence did this awareness come to me? Cer-tainly it did not come "out of the blue." I heard no voice from the skies. No, it came, without a doubt, from what I may call the spiri-tual climate of the home into which I was born. It came from my parents' walk and conversation. At the beginning it may have been merely the consciousness of a conflict between my mother's will and my own, between what I desired and what she desired of me. Yet I cannot profess to remember a time when it was merely that. I cannot remember a time when I did not already dimly know that what opposed my own wilfulness was something much more than mere wilfulness on my mother's part. I knew she had a right to ask of me what she did; which is the same as to say that I knew that what she asked of me was right and that my contrary desire was wrong. I knew, therefore, that my mother's will was not the ulti-mate source of the authority which she exercised over me. For it was plain that she herself was under that same authority. Indeed, it was not only from my parents' specific demands on me that this sense of authority came to me but from the way they themselves lived. Clearly they, too, were under orders, and under essentially the same orders. I cannot remember a time when I did not already know that what my parents demanded of me and what they knew to be demanded of themselves were in the last resort one and the same demand, however different might be its detailed application to our different situations. I cannot remember a time when I did not know that my parents and their household were part of a wider community which was under the same single authority. Nor, again, can I recall a time when I did not know that this authority was closely bound up with, and indeed seemed to emanate from, *a cer-tain story*. As far back as I can remember anything, my parents and my nurses were already speaking to me of Abraham and Isaac and Jacob, of Moses and David, of God's covenant with the Israelites and of their journey through the wilderness, of the culmination of the story in the coming of Jesus Christ, God's only Son, whom He sent to earth to suffer and die for our salvation; and then of the apostles and martyrs and saints and "Scots worthies" whose golden deeds brought the story down to very recent days. And I knew that that story was somehow the source of the authority with which I was confronted. I could not hear a Bible story read without being aware that in it I was somehow being confronted with a solemn presence that had in it both sweetness and rebuke. Nor do I remember a day when I did not already dimly know that this presence was God.

It was, then, through the media of my boyhood's home, the Christian community of which it formed a part, and the "old, old story" from which that community drew its life, that God first revealed Himself to me. This is simple matter of fact. But what I take to be matter of fact in it is not only that God used these media but that in using them He actually did reveal Himself to *my* soul.

For what I seemed to know was not merely that God had declared His will to my parents and that they in their turn had declared their will to me, but also that through my parents God had declared His will to me. The story told me how God had spoken to Abraham and Moses and the prophets and apostles, but what gave the story its power over my mind and imagination and conscience was the knowledge that "in, with and under" this speaking to these others of long ago He was also now speaking to myself. That God should have revealed Himself to certain men of long ago could not in itself be of concern to me now; first, because, not being myself privy to this revelation, I could never know for sure whether it were a real or only an imagined one; second, because mere hearsay could never be a sufficient foundation for such a thing as religion, though it might be well enough as a foundation for certain other kinds of knowledge; and third, because the revelation would necessarily lack the particular authorization and relevance to my case which alone could give it power over my recalcitrant will. What is it to me that God should have commanded David to do this or that, or called Paul to such and such a task? It is nothing at all, unless it should happen that, as I read of His calling and commanding them, I at the same time found Him calling and commanding me.

If the word of God is to concern me, it must be a word addressed to me individually and to the particular concrete situation in which I am standing now. This insight into what we may perhaps venture to call the necessary "here-and-nowness"—the *hic et nunc*—of revelation is one which has emerged very strikingly from recent theological discussions. Kierkegaard's doctrine of the "existential moment" [16] has been a potent influence on many writers; but I need perhaps mention only Dr. Eberhard Grisebach's elaborate demonstration in his book called *Gegenwart*[17] that our sole touch with reality is in the present, the past and the future being alike unreal except so far as they are contained in the present moment.

In a letter to M. de Beaumont, Rousseau once asked, "Is it simple, is it natural, that God should have gone and found Moses in order to speak to Jean Jacques Rousseau?" No, it is far from simple; but what right have we to assume that truth is simple? And as to whether it is natural, have we any knowledge of what would be natural in such a region of experience apart from the witness of the experience itself? We have to take experience as we find it—though that apparently was what Rousseau was refusing to do. And especially we have to face the fact that we have here to do with an experience of an entirely unique kind, its uniqueness lying precisely in this conjunction of immediacy with mediacy—that is, in the fact that God reveals Himself to me only through others who went before, yet in so doing reveals Himself to me now.

This is, indeed, a mysterious ordering of things. Yet I would not be understood as trying to surround it with any spurious air of mystery. Mysterious though it be, it is a mystery with which all men have some degree of acquaintance. It was not *only* in the Bible stories that I was met in my youth with this peculiar conjugation of past and present. Other tales of later days were told me, and in them the same Presence seemed to be speaking to me something of the same word. Were this Presence and this word in *every* tale I was told? I think not. There were, for instance, fairy stories; and they, though they absorbed my interest and caught my imagination,

---

[16] See especially his book *Der Augenblick* (1855).
[17] *Gegenwart, eine Kritische Ethik* (1928).

seemed to have nothing to say to me, nothing to do with me. And of some other stories the same thing was true. The stories that had Presence in them for me, though they were by no means always Bible stories, were somehow of a piece with the Bible stories. Usually, indeed, they were Christian stories, and as such were definitely derivative from the Bible history. But even when that was not the case, if they had Presence in them at all, it was the same Presence as met me in the Bible. And to this day all the history that has Presence in it for me, all the history that has anything to say to me, all of the past through which I am addressed in the present, is centered in the story of the Incarnation and the Cross. All that history has to say to me is somehow related to that; and no story that was entirely out of relation to that could have any present reality in it for me at all. Every story is either B.C. or else A.D.; and that not in mere date but in its very essence; logically as well as chronologically. Indeed, the same story may be chronologically A.D. yet logically B.C., such as stories of noble deeds done within the Christian era by men of other lands whom the knowledge of Christ has not yet reached. Such deeds seem to me to look forward to the Incarnation and the Cross rather than back to them, so that the doers of them are still living as it were under the Old Dispensation. Perhaps these truths of experience on which I have been dwelling have never received better intellectual formulation than in Professor Tillich's doctrine of *die Mitte der Geschichte,* where it is taught that history can have meaning only if it have a centre, and that for the Christian that centre is necessarily Christ. "In dealing with the philosophy of history," he writes, "it is impossible to avoid the Christological problem. History and christology belong to one another as do question and answer." "Instead of the beginning and end of history determining its centre, it is its centre that determines its beginning and end. But the centre of history can only be the place where is revealed the principle that gives it meaning. History is constituted when its centre is constituted, or rather—since this is no mere subjective act—when such a centre reveals its centrality." [18]

[18] *Religiöse Verwirklichung* (1930), pp. 111, 116. The essay from which I quote is translated in *The Interpretation of History* (1936), pp. 242 ff., but I have not followed this somewhat unsatisfactory translation.

The question may now be raised whether a story that has no Presence in it and no word to speak to us really partakes of the true nature of history at all; that is, whether anything can be history for the Christian which does not stand in relation to Christ as its centre. When Dr. Barth insists, as he does so often, that in history in general there is no revelation, since revelation interrupts history at a single point rather than informs it throughout, he is obviously thinking of history as something past and done with. Christ, he says, comes vertically into history and He *alone* reveals God; the history into which He comes does not reveal God *at all*. Thinking of history in this way, the Barthian theologians always oppose "the Christ of Faith" to "the Christ of History." History, they say, cannot give you the truth about Christ; only faith can do that. I believe this dichotomy to be radically mistaken. I believe that a historiographer who writes without faith produces *bad history*. I believe that faith is quite essential to sound historiography. And I believe Professor Tillich's doctrine of Christ as the centre round which all history arranges itself to be altogether profounder than the Barthian attempt to set the rest of history in contrast with Christ. To Professor Tillich history is nothing dead and desiccated, "the presence of the past in the present" being essential to its very nature, so that he can say that in ancient Greek thought "there is no conception of the world as history, even though history as a report on the complex of human movements and as a pattern for politicians be not lacking to it." [19] A similar view is eloquently defended by Dr. Gogarten, to whose treatment of this whole matter I have already acknowledged my debt. "However one may try to solve it," he writes, "and however one may alter its form in so doing, the problem of history is fundamentally the problem of the present-ness of the past. Were the past merely past, as it is in the case of all natural events, there would be no such thing as history but only an unhistorical present—and indeed not even that. For there can be a real present only where there is something past that becomes present." "History is something that happens in the present." [20]

---

[19] *Op. cit.,* p. 112.
[20] *Ich Glaube an den Dreieinigen Gott,* pp. 71 f., 83.

Such, surely, is the right way of it. *It is only in the conception of history as something that happens in the present that the apparent contradiction in our doctrine of a mediated immediacy can be reasonably resolved.*

Instinct, Experience, and Theistic Belief

~~~~~~

Charles Sanders Peirce (1839–1914) was an American astronomer and physicist, as well as one of the founders of the pragmatist tradition in philosophy. His published work is now available in *The Collected Papers of Charles Sanders Peirce*.

492. [We] can know nothing except what we *directly* experience. So all that we can anyway know relates to experience. All the creations of our mind are but patchworks from experience. So that all our ideas are but ideas of real or transposed experiences. A word can mean nothing except the idea it calls up. So that we cannot even *talk* about anything but a knowable object. The unknowable about which Hamilton and the agnostics talk can be nothing but an Unknowable Knowable. The absolutely unknowable is a nonexistent existence. The Unknowable is a nominalistic heresy. The nominalists in giving their adherence to that doctrine which is really held by all philosophers of all stripes, namely, that experience is all we know, understand experience in their nominalistic sense as the mere first

* Reprinted by permission of the publishers from Charles Hartshorne and Paul Weiss, editors, *Collected Papers of Charles Sanders Peirce*, Vol. VI. Cambridge, Mass.: The Belknap Press of Harvard University Press, Copyright, 1935, 1963, by the President and Fellows of Harvard College.

impressions of sense. These "first impressions of sense" are hypothetical creations of nominalistic metaphysics: I for one deny their
existence. But anyway even if they exist, it is not in them that
experience consists. By experience must be understood the entire
mental product. Some psychologists whom I hold in respect will
stop me here to say that, while they admit that experience is more
than mere sensation, they cannot extend it to the whole mental
product, since that would include hallucinations, delusions, superstitious imaginations and fallacies of all kinds; and that they would
limit experience to sense-perceptions. But I reply that my statement
is the logical one. Hallucinations, delusions, superstitious imaginations, and fallacies of all kinds are experiences, but experiences mis-
understood; while to say that all our knowledge relates merely to
sense perception is to say that we can know nothing—not even
mistakenly—about higher matters, as honor, aspirations, and love.

493. Where would such an idea, say as that of God, come from,
if not from direct experience? Would you make it a result of some
kind of reasoning, good or bad? Why, reasoning can supply the
mind with nothing in the world except an estimate of the value of
a statistical ratio, that is, how often certain kinds of things are
found in certain combinations in the ordinary course of experience.
And scepticism, in the sense of doubt of the validity of elementary
ideas—which is really a proposal to turn an idea out of court and
permit no inquiry into its applicability—is doubly condemned by
the fundamental principle of scientific method—condemned first as
obstructing inquiry, and condemned second because it is treating
some other than a statistical ratio as a thing to be argued about.
No: as to God, open your eyes—and your heart, which is also a
perceptive organ—and you see him. But you may ask, Don't you
admit there are any delusions? Yes: I may think a thing is black, and
on close examination it may turn out to be bottle-green. But I cannot think a thing is black if there is no such thing to be seen as
black. Neither can I think that a certain action is self-sacrificing, if
no such thing as self-sacrifice exists, although it may be very rare.
It is the nominalists, and the nominalists alone, who indulge in
such scepticism, which the scientific method utterly condemns.

ANSWERS TO QUESTIONS CONCERNING MY BELIEF IN GOD[1]

1. The Reality of God

494. The questions can be answered without very long explanations. "Do you believe in the existence of a Supreme Being?" Hume, in his *Dialogues Concerning Natural Religion,* justly points out that the phrase "Supreme Being" is not an equivalent of "God," since it neither implies infinity nor any of the other attributes of God, excepting only Being and Supremacy. This is important; and another distinction between the two designations is still more so. Namely, "God" is a vernacular word and, like all such words, but more than almost any, is *vague.* No words are so well understood as vernacular words, in one way; yet they are invariably vague; and of many of them it is true that, let the logician do his best to substitute precise equivalents in their places, still the vernacular words alone, for all their vagueness, answer the principal purposes. This is emphatically the case with the very vague word "God," which is not made less vague by saying that it imports "infinity," and so forth, since those attributes are at least as vague. I shall, therefore, if you please, substitute "God," for "Supreme Being" in the question.

495. I will also take the liberty of substituting "reality" for "existence." This is perhaps overscrupulosity; but I myself always use *exist* in its strict philosophical sense of "react with the other like things in the environment." Of course, in that sense, it would be fetichism to say that God "exists." The word "reality," on the contrary, is used in ordinary parlance in its correct philosophical sense. It is curious that its legal meaning, in which we speak of "real estate," is the earliest, occurring early in the twelfth century. Albertus Magnus, who as a high ecclesiastic, must have had to do with such matters, imported it into philosophy.[2] But it did not become at all common until Duns Scotus, in the latter part of the thirteenth century, began to use it freely.[3] I define the *real* as that

[1] c. 1906.
[2] *Physicorum Liber,* I, 1, I.
[3] See *Sententiarum Libri,* III, Distinctio 34.

which holds its characters on such a tenure that it makes not the slightest difference what any man or men may have *thought* them to be, or ever will have *thought* them to be, here using thought to include, imagining, opining, and willing (as long as forcible *means* are not used); but the real thing's characters will remain absolutely untouched.

496. Of any kind of figment, this is not true. So, then, the question being whether I believe in the reality of God, I answer, Yes. I further opine that pretty nearly everybody more or less believes this, including many of the scientific men of my generation who are accustomed to think the belief is entirely unfounded. The reason they fall into this extraordinary error about their own belief is that they precide (or render precise) the conception, and, in doing so, inevitably change it; and such precise conception is easily shown not to be warranted, even if it cannot be quite refuted. Every concept that is vague is liable to be self-contradictory in those respects in which it is vague. *No* concept, not even those of mathematics, is absolutely precise; and some of the most important for everyday use are extremely vague. Nevertheless, our instinctive beliefs involving such concepts are far more trsutworthy than the best established results of science, if these be precisely understood. For instance, we all think that there is an element of order in the universe. Could any laboratory experiments render that proposition more certain than instinct or common sense leaves it? It is ridiculous to broach such a question. But when anybody undertakes to say *precisely* what that order consists in, he will quickly find he outruns all logical warrant. Men who are given to defining too much inevitably run themselves into confusion in dealing with the vague concepts of common sense.

497. They generally make the matter worse by erroneous, not to say absurd, notions of the function of reasoning. Every race of animals is provided with instincts well adapted to its needs, and especially to strengthening the stock. It is wonderful how unerring these instincts are. Man is no exception in this respect; but man is so continually getting himself into novel situations that he needs, and is supplied with, a subsidiary faculty of *reasoning* for bringing instinct to bear upon situations to which it does not directly apply.

This faculty is a very imperfect one in respect to fallibility; but then it is only needed to bridge short gaps. Every step has to be reviewed and criticized; and indeed this is so essential that it is best to call an uncriticized step of inference by another name. If one does not at all know how one's belief comes about, it cannot be called even by the name of inference. If, with St. Augustine,[4] we draw the inference "I think; therefore, I am," but, when asked how we justify this inference, can only say that we are *compelled to think* that, since we think, we are, this uncriticized inference ought not to be called reasoning, which at the very least conceives its inference to be one of a general class of possible inferences on the same model, and all equally valid. But one must go back and criticize the premisses and the *principles* that guide the drawing of the conclusions. If it could be made out that all the ultimate (or first) premisses were percepts; and that all the ultimate logical principles were as clear as the principle of contradiction, then one might say that one's conclusion was *perfectly* rational. Strictly speaking, it would not be quite so, because it is quite possible for perception itself to deceive us, and it is much more possible for us to be mistaken about the indubitableness of logical principles. But as a matter of fact, as far as logicians have hitherto been able to push their analyses, we have *in no single case,* concerning a matter of *fact,* as distinguished from a matter of mathematical conditional possibility, been able to reach this point. We are in every case either forced by the inexorable critic, sooner or later, to declare, "such and such a proposition or mode of inference *I cannot doubt;* it seems perfectly clear that it is so, but I can't say *why,*" or else the critic himself tires before the criticism has been pushed to its very end.

498. If you absolutely cannot doubt a proposition—cannot bring yourself, upon deliberation, to entertain the least suspicion of the truth of it, it is plain that there is no room to desire anything more. Many and many a philosopher seems to think that taking a piece of paper and writing down "I doubt that" is doubting it, or that it is a thing he can do in a minute as soon as he decides what he wants

---

[4] *De civitate Dei,* XI, 26.

to doubt. Descartes convinced himself that the safest way was to "begin" by doubting everything, and accordingly he tells us he straightway did so, except only his *je pense,* which he borrowed from St. Augustine. Well I guess not; for genuine doubt does not talk of *beginning* with doubting. The pragmatist knows that doubt is an art which has to be acquired with difficulty; and his genuine doubts will go much further than those of any Cartesian. What he does not doubt, about ordinary matters of everybody's life, he is apt to find that no well matured man doubts. They are part of our instincts. Instincts are now known not to be nearly so unchangeable as used to be supposed; and the present "mutation" theory, which I have *always* insisted must be the way in which species have arisen, is, I am confident, the first beginning of the correct theory, and shows that it is no disproof of the instinctive character of a belief that it relates to concepts which the primitive man cannot be supposed to have had. Now, this is no confirmation of what one does not doubt. For what one does not doubt cannot be rendered more satisfactory than it already is. Yet while I may entertain, as far as I can search my mind, no perceptible doubt whatever of any one of a hundred propositions, I may suspect that, among so many, some one that is not true may have slipped in; and, if so, the marvellous inerrancy of instinct may perhaps add a little to my *general* confidence in the whole lot. However, I am far from insisting upon the point. I think the consideration is better adapted to helping us to detect the counterfeit paper doubts, of which so many are in circulation.

499. All the instinctive beliefs, I notice, are vague. The moment they are precided, the pragmatist will begin to doubt them.

500. The fourth part of the first book of Hume's *Treatise of Human Nature* affords a strong argument for the correctness of my view that reason is a mere succedaneum to be used where instinct is wanting, by exhibiting the intensely ridiculous way in which a man winds himself up in silly paper doubts if he undertakes to throw common sense, that is, instinct, overboard and be perfectly rational. Bradley's *Appearance and Reality* is another example of the same thing, although Bradley is at the opposite pole from Hume in what

he *does* admit. But Bradley is in no way as good a case as Hume. Hume endeavours to modify his conclusion by not stating it in the extreme length to which it ought to carry him. But a careful reader will see that if he proves anything at all by all his reasoning, it is that reasoning, as such, is *ipso facto* and essentially illogical, "illegitimate," and unreasonable. And the reason it is so is that either it is bad reasoning, or rests on doubtful premises, or else that those premises have not been thoroughly criticized. Of course not. The moment you come to a proposition which is perfectly satisfactory, so that you can entertain not the smallest suspicion of it, this fact debars you from making any genuine criticism of it. So that what Hume's argument would lead him to is that reasoning is "illegitimate" because its premises are perfectly satisfactory. He candidly confesses that they are satisfactory to himself. But he seems to be dissatisfied with himself for being satisfied. It is easy to see, however, that he pats himself on the back, and is very well satisfied with himself for being so dissatisfied with being satisfied. Bradley's position is equally ridiculous. Another circumstance which goes toward confirming my view that instinct is the great internal source of all wisdom and of all knowledge is that all the "triumphs of science," of which that poor old nineteenth century used to be so vain, have been confined to two directions. They either consist in physical—that is, ultimately, dynamical—explanations of phenomena, or else in explaining things on the basis of our common sense knowledge of human nature. Now dynamics is nothing but an elaboration of common sense; its experiments are mere imaginary experiments. So it all comes down to common sense in these two branches, of which the one is founded on those instincts about physical forces that are required for the feeding impulsion and the other upon those instincts about our fellows that are required for the satisfaction of the reproductive impulse. Thus, then all science is nothing but an outgrowth from these two instincts.

You will see that all I have been saying is not preparatory to any argument for the reality of God. It is intended as an apology for resting the belief upon instinct as the very bedrock on which all reasoning must be built.

501. I have often occasion to walk at night, for about a mile, over an entirely untravelled road, much of it between open fields without a house in sight. The circumstances are not favorable to severe study, but are so to calm meditation. If the sky is clear, I look at the stars in the silence, thinking how each successive increase in the aperture of a telescope makes many more of them visible than all that had been visible before. The fact that the heavens do not show a sheet of light proves that there are vastly more dark bodies, say planets, than there are suns. They must be inhabited, and most likely millions of them with beings much more intelligent than we are. For on the whole, the solar system seems one of the simplest; and presumably under more complicated phenomena greater intellectual power will be developed. What must be the social phenomena of such a world! How extraordinary are the minds even of the lower animals. We cannot appreciate our own powers any more than a writer can appreciate his own style, or a thinker the peculiar quality of his own thought. I don't mean that a Dante did not know that he expressed himself with fewer words than other men do, but he could not admire himself as we admire him; nor can we wonder at human intelligence as we do at that of wasps. Let a man drink in such thoughts as come to him in contemplating the physico-psychical universe without any special purpose of his own; especially the universe of mind which coincides with the universe of matter. The idea of there being a God over it all of course will be often suggested; and the more he considers it, the more he will be enwrapt with Love of this idea. He will ask himself whether or not there really is a God. If he allows instinct to speak, and searches his own heart, he will at length find that he cannot help believing it. I cannot tell how every man will think. I know the majority of men, especially educated men, are so full of pedantries—especially the male sex—that they cannot think straight about these things. But I can tell how a man must think if he is a pragmatist. Now the shower of communications that I have been getting during the last two months causes me to share the expectation that I find so many good judges are entertaining, that pragmatism is going to be the dominant philosophical opinion of the twentieth century. . . .

502. If a pragmaticist is asked what he means by the word "God," he can only say that just as long acquaintance with a man of great character may deeply influence one's whole manner of conduct, so that a glance at his portrait may make a difference, just as almost living with Dr. Johnson enabled poor Boswell to write an immortal book and a really sublime book, just as long study of the works of Aristotle may make him an acquaintance, so if contemplation and study of the physico-psychical universe can imbue a man with principles of conduct analogous to the influence of a great man's works or conversation, then that analogue of a mind—for it is impossible to say that *any* human attribute is *literally* applicable—is what he means by "God." Of course, various great theologians explain that one cannot attribute *reason* to God, nor perception (which always involves an element of surprise and of learning what one did not know), and, in short, that his "mind" is necessarily so unlike ours, that some—though wrongly—high in the church say that it is only negatively, as being entirely different from everything else, that we can attach any meaning to the Name. This is not so; because the discoveries of science, their enabling us to *predict* what will be the course of nature, is proof conclusive that, though we cannot think any thought of God's, we can catch a fragment of His Thought, as it were.

503. Now such being the pragmaticist's answer to the question what he means by the word "God," the question whether there really *is* such a being is the question whether all physical science is merely the figment—the arbitrary figment—of the students of nature, and further whether the *one* lesson the Gautama Boodha, Confucius, Socrates, and all who from any point of view have had their ways of conduct determined by meditation upon the physico-psychical universe, be only their arbitrary notion or be the Truth behind the appearances which the frivolous man does not think of; and whether the superhuman courage which such contemplation has conferred upon priests who go to pass their lives with lepers and refuse all offers of rescue is mere silly fanaticism, the passion of a baby, or whether it is strength derived from the power of the truth. Now the only guide to the answer to this question lies in the

power of the passion of love which more or less overmasters every agnostic scientist and everybody who seriously and deeply considers the universe. But whatever there may be of *argument* in all this is as nothing, the merest nothing, in comparison to its force as an appeal to one's own instinct, which is to argument what substance is to shadow, what bedrock is to the built foundations of a cathedral.

WILLIAM K. CLIFFORD

The Ethics of Belief

William K. Clifford (1845–1879) was a British mathematician with philosophical interests. His main works of philosophical importance are *Lectures and Essays, Seeing and Thinking,* and *Common Sense of the Exact Sciences.*

A shipowner was about to send to sea an emigrant ship. He knew that she was old, and not over-well built at the first; that she had seen many seas and climes, and often had needed repairs. Doubts had been suggested to him that possibly she was not seaworthy. These doubts preyed upon his mind, and made him unhappy; he thought that perhaps he ought to have her thoroughly overhauled and refitted, even though this should put him to great expense. Before the ship sailed, however, he succeeded in overcoming these melancholy reflections. He said to himself that she had gone safely through so many voyages and weathered so many storms that it was idle to suppose she would not come safely home from this trip also. He would put his trust in Providence, which could hardly fail to protect all these unhappy families that were leaving their fatherland to seek for better times elsewhere. He would dismiss from his mind all ungenerous suspicions about the honesty of builders and con-

* Reprinted from W. K. Clifford, *Lectures and Essays.*

tractors. In such ways he acquired a sincere and comfortable conviction that his vessel was thoroughly safe and seaworthy; he watched her departure with a light heart, and benevolent wishes for the success of the exiles in their strange new home that was to be; and he got his insurance money when she went down in mid-ocean and told no tales.

What shall we say of him? Surely this, that he was verily guilty of the death of those men. It is admitted that he did sincerely believe in the soundness of his ship; but the sincerity of his conviction can in no wise help him, because *he had no right to believe on such evidence as was before him.* He had acquired his belief not by honestly earning it in patient investigation, but by stifling his doubts. And although in the end he may have felt so sure about it that he could not think otherwise, yet inasmuch as he had knowingly and willingly worked himself into that frame of mind, he must be held responsible for it.

Let us alter the case a little, and suppose that the ship was not unsound after all; that she made her voyage safely, and many others after it. Will that diminish the guilt of her owner? Not one jot. When an action is once done, it is right or wrong for ever; no accidental failure of its good or evil fruits can possibly alter that. The man would not have been innocent, he would only have been not found out. The question of right or wrong has to do with the origin of his belief, not the matter of it; not what it was, but how he got it; not whether it turned out to be true or false, but whether he had a right to believe on such evidence as was before him.

There was once an island in which some of the inhabitants professed a religion teaching neither the doctrine of original sin nor that of eternal punishment. A suspicion got abroad that the professors of this religion had made use of unfair means to get their doctrines taught to children. They were accused of wresting the laws of their country in such a way as to remove children from the care of their natural and legal guardians; and even of stealing them away and keeping them concealed from their friends and relations. A certain number of men formed themselves into a society for the purpose of agitating the public about this matter. They published grave accusations against individual citizens of the highest position and character, and did all in their power to injure these citizens in the exercise of their professions. So great was the noise they made, that a Commission was appointed to investigate the facts; but after the Commission had carefully inquired into all the evidence that could be got, it appeared that the accused were innocent. Not only had they been accused on insufficient evidence, but the evidence of their innocence was such as the agitators might easily have obtained, if they had attempted a fair inquiry. After these disclosures the inhabitants of that country looked upon the members of the agitating society, not only as persons whose judgment was to be distrusted, but also as no longer to be counted honourable men. For although they had sincerely and conscientiously believed in the charges they had made, yet *they had no right to believe on such evidence as was before them.* Their sincere convictions, instead of being honestly earned by patient inquiring, were stolen by listening to the voice of prejudice and passion.

Let us vary this case also, and suppose, other things remaining as before, that a still more accurate investigation proved the accused to have been really guilty. Would this make any difference in the guilt of the accusers? Clearly not; the question is not whether their belief was true or false, but whether they entertained it on wrong grounds. They would no doubt say, "Now you see that we were right after all; next time perhaps you will believe us." And they might be believed, but they would not thereby become honourable men. They would not be innocent, they would only be not found out. Every one of them, if he chose to examine himself *in foro conscientiæ,* would know that he had acquired and nourished a belief, when he had no right to believe on such evidence as was before him; and therein he would know that he had done a wrong thing.

It may be said, however, that in both of these supposed cases it is not the belief which is judged to be wrong, but the action following upon it. The shipowner might say, "I am perfectly certain that my ship is sound, but still I feel it my duty to have her examined, before trusting the lives of so many people to her." And it might be said to the agitator, "However convinced you were of the justice of your cause and the truth of your convictions, you ought not to have made a public attack upon any man's character until you had examined the evidence on both sides with the utmost patience and care."

In the first place, let us admit that, so far as it goes, this view of the case is right and necessary; right, because even when a man's belief is so fixed that he cannot think otherwise, he still has a choice in regard to the action suggested by it, and so cannot escape the duty of investigating on the ground of the strength of his convictions; and necessary, because those who are not yet capable of controlling their feelings and thoughts must have a plain rule dealing with overt acts.

But this being premised as necessary, it becomes clear that it is not sufficient, and that our previous judgment is required to supplement it. For it is not possible so to sever the belief from the action it suggests as to condemn the one without condemning the other. No man holding a strong belief on one side of a question, or even wishing to hold a belief on one side, can investigate it with such fairness and completeness as if he were really in doubt and unbiassed; so that the existence of a belief not founded on fair inquiry unfits a man for the performance of this necessary duty.

Nor is that truly a belief at all which has not some influence upon the actions of him who holds it. He who truly believes that which prompts him to an action has looked upon the action to lust after it, he has committed it already in his heart. If a belief is not realized immediately in open deeds, it is stored up for the guidance of the future. It goes to make a part of that aggregate of beliefs which is the link between sensation and action at every moment of all our lives, and which is so organized and compacted together that no part of it can be isolated from the rest, but every new addition modifies the structure of the whole. No real belief, however trifling and fragmentary it may seem, is ever truly insignificant; it prepares us to receive more of its like, confirms those which resembled it before, and weakens others; and so gradually it lays a stealthy train in our inmost thoughts, which may some day explode into overt action, and leave its stamp upon our character for ever.

And no one man's belief is in any case a private matter which concerns himself alone. Our lives are guided by that general conception of the course of things which has been created by society for social purposes. Our words, our phrases, our forms and processes and modes of thought, are common property, fashioned and perfected from age to age; an heirloom which every succeeding generation inherits as a precious deposit and a sacred trust to be handed on to the next one, not unchanged but enlarged and purified, with some clear marks of its proper handiwork. Into this, for good or ill, is woven every belief of every man who has speech of his fellows. An awful privilege, and an awful responsibility, that we should help to create the world in which posterity will live.

In the two supposed cases which have been considered, it has been judged wrong to believe on insufficient evidence, or to nourish belief by suppressing doubts and avoiding investigation. The reason of this judgment is not far to seek: it is that in both these cases the belief held by one man was of great importance to other men. But forasmuch as no belief held by one man, however seemingly trivial the belief, and however obscure the believer, is ever actually insignificant or without its effect on the fate of mankind, we have no choice but to extend our judgment to all cases of belief whatever. Belief, that sacred faculty which prompts the decisions of our will, and knits into harmonious working all the compacted energies of our being, is ours not for ourselves, but for humanity. It is rightly used on truths which have been established by long experience and waiting toil, and which have stood in the fierce light of free and fearless questioning. Then it helps to bind men together, and to strengthen and direct their common action. It is desecrated when given to unproved and unquestioned statements, for the solace and private pleasure of the believer; to add a tinsel splendour to the plain straight road of our life and display a bright mirage beyond it; or even to drown the common sorrows of our kind by a self-deception which allows them not only to cast down, but also to degrade us. Whoso would deserve well of his fellows in this matter will guard the purity of his belief with a very fanaticism of jealous care, lest at any time it should rest on an unworthy object, and catch a stain which can never be wiped away.

It is not only the leader of men, statesman, philosopher, or poet, that owes this bounden duty to mankind. Every rustic who delivers in the village alehouse his slow, infrequent sentences, may help to kill or keep alive the fatal superstitions which clog his race. Every hard-worked wife of an artisan may transmit to her children beliefs which shall knit society together, or rend it in pieces. No simplicity of mind, no obscurity of station, can escape the universal duty of questioning all that we believe.

It is true that this duty is a hard one, and the doubt which comes out of it is often a very bitter thing. It leaves us bare and powerless where we thought that we were safe and strong. To know all about anything is to know how to deal with it under all circumstances. We feel much happier and more secure when we think we know precisely what to do, no matter what happens, than when we have lost our way and do not know where to turn. And if we have sup- posed ourselves to know all about anything, and to be capable of doing what is fit in regard to it, we naturally do not like to find that we are really ignorant and powerless, that we have to begin again at the beginning, and try to learn what the thing is and how it is to be dealt with—if indeed anything can be learnt about it. It is the sense of power attached to a sense of knowledge that makes men desirous of believing, and afraid of doubting.

The sense of power is the highest and best of pleasures when the belief on which it is founded is a true belief, and has been fairly earned by investigation. For then we may justly feel that it is common property, and holds good for others as well as for ourselves. Then we may be glad, not that *I* have learned secrets by which I am safer and stronger, but that *we men* have got mastery over more of the world; and we shall be strong, not for ourselves, but in the name of Man and in his strength. But if the belief has been accepted on insufficient evidence, the pleasure is a stolen one. Not only does it deceive ourselves by giving us a sense of power which we do not really possess, but it is sinful, because it is stolen in defiance of our duty to mankind. That duty is to guard ourselves from such beliefs as from a pestilence, which may shortly master our own body and then spread to the rest of the town. What would be thought of one who, for the sake of a sweet fruit, should deliberately run the risk of bringing a plague upon his family and his neighbours?

And, as in other such cases, it is not the risk only which has to be considered; for a bad action is always bad at the time when it is done, no matter what happens afterwards. Every time we let ourselves believe for unworthy reasons, we weaken our powers of self-control, of doubting, of judicially and fairly weighing evidence. We all suffer severely enough from the maintenance and support of false beliefs and the fatally wrong actions which they lead to, and the evil born when one such belief is entertained is great and wide. But a greater and wider evil arises when the credulous character is maintained and supported, when a habit of believing for unworthy reasons is fostered and made permanent. If I steal money from any person, there may be no harm done by the mere transfer of possession; he may not feel the loss, or it may prevent him from using the money badly. But I cannot help doing this great wrong towards Man, that I make myself dishonest. What hurts society is not that it should lose its property, but that it should become a den of thieves; for then it must cease to be society. This is why we ought not to do evil that good may come; for at any rate this great evil has come, that we have done evil and are made wicked thereby. In like manner, if I let myself believe anything on insufficient evidence, there may be no great harm done by the mere belief; it may be true after all, or I may never have occasion to exhibit it in outward acts. But I cannot help doing this great wrong towards Man, that I make myself credulous. The danger to society is not merely that it should believe wrong things, though that is great enough; but that it should become credulous, and lose the habit of testing things and inquiring into them; for then it must sink back into savagery.

The harm which is done by credulity in a man is not confined to the fostering of a credulous character in others, and consequent support of false beliefs. Habitual want of care about what I believe leads to habitual want of care in others about the truth of what is told to me. Men speak the truth to one another when each reveres the truth in his own mind and in the other's mind; but how shall my friend revere the truth in my mind when I myself am careless about it, when I believe things because I want to believe them, and because they are comforting and pleasant? Will he not learn to cry, "Peace," to me, when there is no peace? By such a course I shall surround myself with a thick atmosphere of falsehood and fraud, and in that I must live. It may matter little to me, in my cloud-castle of sweet illusions and darling lies; but it matters much to Man that I have made my neighbours ready to deceive. The credulous man is father to the liar and the cheat; he lives in the bosom of this his family, and it is no marvel if he should become even as they are. So closely are our duties knit together, that whoso shall keep the whole law, and yet offend in one point, he is guilty of all.

To sum up: it is wrong always, everywhere, and for anyone, to believe anything upon insufficient evidence.

If a man, holding a belief which he was taught in childhood or persuaded of afterwards, keeps down and pushes away any doubts which arise about it in his mind, purposely avoids the reading of books and the company of men that call in question or discuss it, and regards as impious those questions which cannot easily be asked without disturbing it—the life of that man is one long sin against mankind.

If this judgment seems harsh when applied to those simple souls who have never known better, who have been brought up from the cradle with a horror of doubt, and taught that their eternal welfare depends on *what* they believe, then it leads to the very serious question, *Who hath made Israel to sin?*

It may be permitted me to fortify this judgment with the sentence of Milton:[1]

"A man may be a heretic in the truth; and if he believe things only because his pastor says so, or the assembly so determine, without knowing other reason, though his belief be true, yet the very truth he holds becomes his heresy."

And with this famous aphorism of Coleridge:[2]

"He who begins by loving Christianity better than Truth, will proceed by loving his own sect or Church better than Christianity, and end in loving himself better than all."

Inquiry into the evidence of a doctrine is not to be made once for

[1] *Areopagitica.*
[2] *Aids to Reflection.*

all, and then taken as finally settled. It is never lawful to stifle a doubt; for either it can be honestly answered by means of the inquiry already made, or else it proves that the inquiry was not complete.

"But," says one, "I am a busy man; I have no time for the long course of study which would be necessary to make me in any degree a competent judge of certain questions, or even able to understand the nature of the arguments." Then he should have no time to believe.

WILLIAM JAMES

The Will to Believe

William James (1842–1910) was a leading American pragmatist philosopher, as well as a psychologist. Some of his best-known books are *Principles of Psychology, Varieties of Religious Experience,* and *Pragmatism: A New Name for Some Old Ways of Thinking.*

In the recently published Life by Leslie Stephen of his brother, Fitz-James, there is an account of a school to which the latter went when he was a boy. The teacher, a certain Mr. Guest, used to converse with his pupils in this wise: "Gurney, what is the difference between justification and sanctification?—Stephen, prove the omnipotence of God!" and so forth. In the midst of our Harvard freethinking and indifference we are prone to imagine that here at your good old orthodox College conversation continues to be somewhat upon this order; and to show you that we at Harvard have not lost all interest in these vital subjects, I have brought with me tonight something like a sermon on justification by faith to read to you,—I mean an essay in justification *of* faith, a defence of our right to adopt a believing attitude in religious matters, in spite of the fact that our merely logical intellect may not have been coerced. "The Will to Believe," accordingly, is the title of my paper.

* From W. James, *The Will to Believe and Other Essays.*

I have long defended to my own students the lawfulness of voluntarily adopted faith; but as soon as they have got well imbued with the logical spirit, they have as a rule refused to admit my contention to be lawful philosophically, even though in point of fact they were personally all the time chock-full of some faith or other themselves. I am all the while, however, so profoundly convinced that my own position is correct, that your invitation has seemed to me a good occasion to make my statements more clear. Perhaps your minds will be more open than those with which I have hitherto had to deal. I will be as little technical as I can, though I must begin by setting up some technical distinctions that will help us in the end.

I

Let us give the name of *hypothesis* to anything that may be proposed to our belief; and just as the electricians speak of live and dead wires, let us speak of any hypothesis as either *live* or *dead*. A live hypothesis is one which appeals as a real possibility to him to whom it is proposed. If I ask you to believe in the Mahdi, the notion makes no electric connection with your nature—it refuses to scintillate with any credibility at all. As an hypothesis it is completely dead. To an Arab, however (even if he be not one of the Mahdi's followers), the hypothesis is among the mind's possibilities: it is alive. This shows that deadness and liveness in an hypothesis are not intrinsic properties, but relations to the individual thinker. They are measured by his willingness to act. The maximum of liveness in an hypothesis means willingness to act irrevocably. Practically, that means belief; but there is some believing tendency wherever there is willingness to act at all.

Next, let us call the decision between two hypotheses an *option*. Options may be of several kinds. They may be (1) *living* or *dead;* (2) *forced* or *avoidable;* (3) *momentous* or *trivial;* and for our purposes we may call an option a *genuine* option when it is of the forced, living, and momentous kind.

(1) A living option is one in which both hypotheses are live ones. If I say to you: "Be a theosophist or be a Mohammedan," it is prob-

ably a dead option, because for you neither hypothesis is likely to be alive. But if I say: "Be an agnostic or be a Christian," it is otherwise: trained as you are, each hypothesis makes some appeal, however small, to your belief.

(2) Next, if I say to you: "Choose between going out with your umbrella or without it," I do not offer you a genuine option, for it is not forced. You can easily avoid it by not going out at all. Similarly, if I say, "Either love me or hate me," "Either call my theory true or call it false," your option is avoidable. You may remain indifferent to me, neither loving nor hating, and you may decline to offer any judgment as to my theory. But if I say, "Either accept this truth or go without it," I put on you a forced option, for there is no standing place outside of the alternative. Every dilemma based on a complete logical disjunction, with no possibility of not choosing, is an option of this forced kind.

(3) Finally, if I were Dr. Nansen and proposed to you to join my North Pole expedition, your option would be momentous; for this would probably be your only similar opportunity, and your choice now would either exclude you from the North Pole sort of immortality altogether or put at least the chance of it into your hands. He who refuses to embrace a unique opportunity loses the prize as surely as if he tried and failed. *Per contra,* the option is trivial when the opportunity is not unique, when the stake is insignificant, or when the decision is reversible if it later prove unwise. Such trivial options abound in the scientific life. A chemist finds an hypothesis live enough to spend a year in its verification: he believes in it to that extent. But if his experiments prove inconclusive either way, he is quit for his loss of time, no vital harm being done.

It will facilitate our discussion if we keep all these distinctions well in mind.

II

The next matter to consider is the actual psychology of human opinion. When we look at certain facts, it seems as if our passional and volitional nature lay at the root of all our convictions. When we look at others, it seems as if they could do nothing when the intellect had once said its say. Let us take the latter facts up first.

Does it not seem preposterous on the very face of it to talk of our opinions being modifiable at will? Can our will either help or hinder our intellect in its perceptions of truth? Can we, by just willing it, believe that Abraham Lincoln's existence is a myth, and that the portraits of him in McClure's Magazine are all of some one else? Can we, by any effort of our will, or by any strength of wish that it were true, believe ourselves well and about when we are roaring with rheumatism in bed, or feel certain that the sum of the two one-dollar bills in our pocket must be a hundred dollars? We can *say* any of these things, but we are absolutely impotent to believe them; and of just such things is the whole fabric of the truths that we do believe in made up,—matters of fact, immediate or remote, as Hume said, and relations between ideas, which are either there or not there for us if we see them so, and which if not there cannot be put there by any action of our own.

In Pascal's *Thoughts* there is a celebrated passage known in literature as *Pascal's wager*. In it he tries to force us into Christianity by reasoning as if our concern with truth resembled our concern with the stakes in a game of chance. Translated freely his words are these: You must either believe or not believe that God is— which will you do? Your human reason cannot say. A game is going on between you and the nature of things which at the day of judgment will bring out either heads or tails. Weigh what your gains and your losses would be if you should stake all you have on heads, or God's existence: if you win in such case, you gain eternal beatitude; if you lose, you lose nothing at all. If there were an infinity of chances, and only one for God in this wager, still you ought to stake your all on God; for though you surely risk a finite loss by this procedure, any finite loss is reasonable, even a certain one is reasonable, if there is but the possibility of infinite gain. Go, then, and take holy water, and have masses said; belief will come and stupefy your scruples—*Cela vous fera croire et vous abêtira.* Why should you not? At bottom, what have you to lose?

You probably feel that when religious faith expresses itself thus, in the language of the gaming table, it is put to its last trumps.

Surely Pascal's own personal belief in masses and holy water had far other springs; and this celebrated page of his is but an argument for others, a last desperate snatch at a weapon against the hardness of the unbelieving heart. We feel that a faith in masses and holy water adopted wilfully after such a mechanical calculation would lack the inner soul of faith's reality; and if we were ourselves in the place of the Deity, we should probably take particular pleasure in cutting off believers of this pattern from their infinite reward. It is evident that unless there be some pre-existing tendency to believe in masses and holy water, the option offered to the will by Pascal is not a living option. Certainly no Turk ever took to masses and holy water on its account; and even to us Protestants these means of salvation seem such foregone impossibilities that Pascal's logic, invoked for them specifically, leaves us unmoved. As well might the Mahdi write to us, saying, "I am the Expected One whom God has created in his effulgence. You shall be infinitely happy if you confess me; otherwise you shall be cut off from the light of the sun. Weigh, then, your infinite gain if I am genuine against your finite sacrifice if I am not!" His logic would be that of Pascal; but he would vainly use it on us, for the hypothesis he offers us is dead. No tendency to act on it exists in us to any degree.

The talk of believing by our volition seems, then, from one point of view, simply silly. From another point of view it is worse than silly, it is vile. When one turns to the magnificent edifice of the physical sciences, and sees how it was reared; what thousands of disinterested moral lives of men lie buried in its mere foundations; what patience and postponement, what choking down of preference, what submission to the icy laws of outer fact are wrought into its very stones and mortar; how absolutely impersonal it stands in its vast augustness—then how besotted and contemptible seems every little sentimentalist who comes blowing his voluntary smoke-wreaths, and pretending to decide things from out of his private dream! Can we wonder if those bred in the rugged and manly school of science should feel like spewing such subjectivism out of their mouths? The whole system of loyalties which grow up in the schools of science go dead against its toleration; so that it is only natural that those who have caught the scientific fever should pass over to the opposite extreme, and write sometimes as if the incorruptibly truthful intellect ought positively to prefer bitterness and unacceptableness to the heart in its cup.

> It fortifies my soul to know
> That, though I perish, Truth is so—

sings Clough, while Huxley exclaims: "My only consolation lies in the reflection that, however bad our posterity may become, so far as they hold by the plain rule of not pretending to believe what they have no reason to believe, because it may be to their advantage so to pretend [the word 'pretend' is surely here redundant], they will not have reached the lowest depth of immorality." And that delicious *enfant terrible* Clifford writes: "Belief is desecrated when given to unproved and unquestioned statements for the solace and private pleasure of the believer. . . . Whoso would deserve well of his fellows in this matter will guard the purity of his belief with a very fanaticism of jealous care, lest at any time it should rest on an unworthy object, and catch a stain which can never be wiped away. . . . If [a] belief has been accepted on insufficient evidence [even though the belief be true, as Clifford on the same page explains] the pleasure is a stolen one. . . . It is sinful because it is stolen in defiance of our duty to mankind. That duty is to guard ourselves from such beliefs as from a pestilence which may shortly master our own body and then spread to the rest of the town. . . . It is wrong always, everywhere, and for every one, to believe anything upon insufficient evidence."

III

All this strikes one as healthy, even when expressed, as by Clifford, with somewhat too much of robustious pathos in the voice. Free will and simple wishing do seem, in the matter of our credences, to be only fifth wheels to the coach. Yet if any one should thereupon assume that intellectual insight is what remains after wish and will and sentimental preference have taken wing, or that pure reason is what then settles our opinions, he would fly quite as directly in the teeth of the facts.

It is only our already dead hypotheses that our willing nature is

unable to bring to life again. But what has made them dead for
us is for the most part a previous action of our willing nature of
an antagonistic kind. When I say "willing nature," I do not mean
only such deliberate volitions as may have set up habits of belief
that we cannot now escape from—I mean all such factors of belief
as fear and hope, prejudice and passion, imitation and partisanship,
the circumpressure of our caste and set. As a matter of fact we find
ourselves believing, we hardly know how or why. Mr. Balfour gives
the name of "authority" to all those influences, born of the intellectual climate, that make hypotheses possible or impossible for us,
alive or dead. Here in this room, we all of us believe in molecules
and the conservation of energy, in democracy and necessary progress, in Protestant Christianity and the duty of fighting for "the
doctrine of the immortal Monroe," all for no reasons worthy of the
name. We see into these matters with no more inner clearness, and
probably with much less, than any disbeliever in them might possess. His unconventionality would probably have some grounds to
show for its conclusions; but for us, not insight, but the *prestige*
of the opinions, is what makes the spark shoot from them and light
up our sleeping magazines of faith. Our reason is quite satisfied,
in nine hundred and ninety-nine cases out of every thousand of us,
if it can find a few arguments that will do to recite in case our
credulity is criticised by some one else. Our faith is faith in some
one else's faith, and in the greatest matters this is most the case.
Our belief in truth itself, for instance, that there is a truth, and
that our minds and it are made for each other—what is it but a
passionate affirmation of desire, in which our social system backs us
up? We want to have a truth; we want to believe that our experiments and studies and discussions must put us in a continually
better and better position towards it; and on this line we agree to
fight out our thinking lives. But if a pyrrhonistic sceptic asks us *how
we know* all this, can our logic find a reply? No! certainly it cannot.
It is just one volition against another—we willing to go in for life
upon a trust or assumption which he, for his part, does not care to
make.[1]

As a rule we disbelieve all facts and theories for which we have

[1] Compare the admirable page 310 in S. H. Hodgson's "Time and Space,"
London, 1865.

no use. Clifford's cosmic emotions find no use for Christian feelings. Huxley belabors the bishops because there is no use for sacerdotalism in his scheme of life. Newman, on the contrary, goes over to Romanism, and finds all sorts of reasons good for staying there, because a priestly system is for him an organic need and delight. Why do so few "scientists" even look at the evidence for telepathy, so called? Because they think, as a leading biologist, now dead, once said to me, that even if such a thing were true, scientists ought to band together to keep it suppressed and concealed. It would undo the uniformity of Nature and all sorts of other things without which scientists cannot carry on their pursuits. But if this very man had been shown something which as a scientist he might *do* with telepathy, he might not only have examined the evidence, but even have found it good enough. This very law which the logicians would impose upon us—if I may give the name of logicians to those who would rule out our willing nature here—is based on nothing but their own natural wish to exclude all elements for which they, in their professional quality of logicians, can find no use.

Evidently, then, our nonintellectual nature does influence our convictions. There are passional tendencies and volitions which run before and others which come after belief, and it is only the latter that are too late for the fair; and they are not too late when the previous passional work has been already in their own direction. Pascal's argument, instead of being powerless, then seems a regular clincher, and is the last stroke needed to make our faith in masses and holy water complete. The state of things is evidently far from simple; and pure insight and logic, whatever they might do ideally, are not the only things that really do produce our creeds.

IV

Our next duty, having recognized this mixed-up state of affairs, is to ask whether it be simply reprehensible and pathological, or whether, on the contrary, we must treat it as a normal element in making up our minds. The thesis I defend is, briefly stated, this: *Our passional nature not only lawfully may, but must, decide an*

*option between propositions, whenever it is a genuine option that
cannot by its nature be decided on intellectual grounds; for to
say, under such circumstances, "Do not decide, but leave the question open," is itself a passional decision—just like deciding yes or
no—and is attended with the same risk of losing the truth.* The
thesis thus abstractly expressed will, I trust, soon become quite clear.
But I must first indulge in a bit more of preliminary work.

V

It will be observed that for the purposes of this discussion we are
on "dogmatic" ground—ground, I mean, which leaves systematic
philosophical scepticism altogether out of account. The postulate
that there is truth, and that it is the destiny of our minds to attain
it, we are deliberately resolving to make, though the sceptic will
not make it. We part company with him, therefore, absolutely,
at this point. But the faith that truth exists, and that our minds
can find it, may be held in two ways. We may talk of the *empiricist*
way and of the *absolutist* way of believing in truth. The absolutists
in this matter say that we not only can attain to knowing truth,
but we can *know when* we have attained to knowing it; while the
empiricists think that although we may attain it, we cannot in-
fallibly know when. To *know* is one thing, and to know for certain
that we know is another. One may hold to the first being possible
without the second; hence the empiricists and the absolutists, although neither of them is a sceptic in the usual philosophic sense
of the term, show very different degrees of dogmatism in their lives.

If we look at the history of opinions, we see that the empiricist
tendency has largely prevailed in science, while in philosophy the
absolutist tendency has had everything its own way. The characteristic sort of happiness, indeed, which philosophies yield has
mainly consisted in the conviction felt by each successive school
or system that by it bottom-certitude had been attained. "Other
philosophies are collections of opinions, mostly false; *my* philosophy
gives standing-ground forever"—who does not recognize in this
the keynote of every system worthy of the name? A system, to be a

system at all, must come as a *closed* system, reversible in this or that detail, perchance, but in its essential features never!

Scholastic orthodoxy, to which one must always go when one wishes to find perfectly clear statement, has beautifully elaborated this absolutist conviction in a doctrine which it calls that of "objective evidence." If, for example, I am unable to doubt that I now exist before you, that two is less than three, or that if all men are mortal then I am mortal too, it is because these things illumine my intellect irresistibly. The final ground of this objective evidence possessed by certain propositions is the *adæquatio intellectûs nostri cum rê.* The certitude it brings involves an *aptitudinem ad extorquendum certum assensum* on the part of the truth envisaged, and on the side of the subject a *quietem in cognitione,* when once the object is mentally received, that leaves no possibility of doubt behind; and in the whole transaction nothing operates but the *entitas ipsa* of the object and the *entitas ipsa* of the mind. We slouchy modern thinkers dislike to talk in Latin—indeed, we dislike to talk in set terms at all; but at bottom our own state of mind is very much like this whenever we uncritically abandon ourselves: You believe in objective evidence, and I do. Of some things we feel that we are certain: we know, and we know that we do know. There is something that gives a click inside of us, a bell that strikes twelve, when the hands of our mental clock have swept the dial and meet over the meridian hour. The greatest empiricists among us are only empiricists on reflection: when left to their instincts, they dogmatize like infallible popes. When the Cliffords tell us how sinful it is to be Christians on such "insufficient evidence," insufficiency is really the last thing they have in mind. For them the evidence is absolutely sufficient, only it makes the other way. They believe so completely in an antichristian order of the universe that there is no living option: Christianity is a dead hypothesis from the start.

VI

But now, since we are all such absolutists by instinct, what in our quality of students of philosophy ought we to do about the fact?

Shall we espouse and indorse it? Or shall we treat it as a weakness of our nature from which we must free ourselves, if we can?

I sincerely believe that the latter course is the only one we can follow as reflective men. Objective evidence and certitude are doubtless very fine ideals to play with, but where on this moonlit and dream-visited planet are they found? I am, therefore, myself a complete empiricist so far as my theory of human knowledge goes. I live, to be sure, by the practical faith that we must go on experiencing and thinking over our experience, for only thus can our opinions grow more true; but to hold any one of them—I absolutely do not care which—as if it never could be reinterpretable or corrigible, I believe to be a tremendously mistaken attitude, and I think that the whole history of philosophy will bear me out. There is but one indefectibly certain truth, and that is the truth that pyrrhonistic scepticism itself leaves standing—the truth that the present phenomenon of consciousness exists. That, however, is the bare starting point of knowledge, the mere admission of a stuff to be philosophized about. The various philosophies are but so many attempts at expressing what this stuff really is. And if we repair to our libraries what disagreement do we discover! Where is a certainly true answer found? Apart from abstract propositions of comparison (such as two and two are the same as four), propositions which tell us nothing by themselves about concrete reality, we find no proposition ever regarded by any one as evidently certain that has not either been called a falsehood, or at least had its truth sincerely questioned by some one else. The transcending of the axioms of geometry, not in play but in earnest, by certain of our contemporaries (as Zöllner and Charles H. Hinton), and the rejection of the whole Aristotelian logic by the Hegelians, are striking instances in point.

No concrete test of what is really true has ever been agreed upon. Some make the criterion external to the moment of perception, putting it either in revelation, the *consensus gentium,* the instincts of the heart, or the systematized experience of the race. Others make the perceptive moment its own test—Descartes, for instance, with his clear and distinct ideas guaranteed by the veracity of God; Reid with his "common-sense"; and Kant with his forms of synthetic judgment *a priori*. The inconceivability of the opposite; the capacity to be verified by sense; the possession of complete organic unity or self-relation, realized when a thing is its own other—are standards which, in turn, have been used. The much lauded objective evidence is never triumphantly there; it is a mere aspiration or *Grenzbegriff*, marking the infinitely remote ideal of our thinking life. To claim that certain truths now possess it, is simply to say that when you think them true and they *are* true, then their evidence is objective, otherwise it is not. But practically one's conviction that the evidence one goes by is of the real objective brand, is only one more subjective opinion added to the lot. For what a contradictory array of opinions have objective evidence and absolute certitude been claimed! The world is rational through and through—its existence is an ultimate brute fact; there is a personal God—a personal God is inconceivable; there is an extra-mental physical world immediately known—the mind can only know its own ideas; a moral imperative exists—obligation is only the resultant of desires; a permanent spiritual principle is in every one—there are only shifting states of mind; there is an endless chain of causes—there is an absolute first cause; an eternal necessity—a freedom; a purpose—no purpose; a primal One—a primal Many; a universal continuity—an essential discontinuity in things; an infinity—no infinity. There is this—there is that; there is indeed nothing which some one has not thought absolutely true, while his neighbor deemed it absolutely false; and not an absolutist among them seems ever to have considered that the trouble may all the time be essential, and that the intellect, even with truth directly in its grasp, may have no infallible signal for knowing whether it be truth or no. When, indeed, one remembers that the most striking practical application to life of the doctrine of objective certitude has been the conscientious labors of the Holy Office of the Inquisition, one feels less tempted than ever to lend the doctrine a respectful ear.

But please observe, now, that when as empiricists we give up the doctrine of objective certitude, we do not thereby give up the quest or hope of truth itself. We still pin our faith on its existence, and still believe that we gain an ever better position towards it by systematically continuing to roll up experiences and think. Our great difference from the scholastic lies in the way we face. The strength of his system lies in the principles, the origin, the *terminus a quo* of his thought; for us the strength is in the outcome, the upshot, the *terminus ad quem.* Not where it comes from but what it leads to is to decide. It matters not to an empiricist from what quarter an hypothesis may come to him: he may have acquired it by fair means or by foul; passion may have whispered or accident suggested it; but if the total drift of thinking continues to confirm it, that is what he means by its being true.

VII

One more point, small but important, and our preliminaries are done. There are two ways of looking at our duty in the matter of opinion—ways entirely different, and yet ways about whose difference the theory of knowledge seems hitherto to have shown very little concern. *We must know the truth;* and *we must avoid error*—these are our first and great commandments as would-be knowers; but they are not two ways of stating an identical commandment, they are two separable laws. Although it may indeed happen that when we believe the truth *A*, we escape as an incidental consequence from believing the falsehood *B*, it hardly ever happens that by merely disbelieving *B* we necessarily believe *A*. We may in escaping *B* fall into believing other falsehoods, *C* or *D*, just as bad as *B*; or we may escape *B* by not believing anything at all, not even *A*.

Believe truth! Shun error! these, we see, are two materially different laws; and by choosing between them we may end by coloring differently our whole intellectual life. We may regard the chase for truth as paramount, and the avoidance of error as secondary; or we may, on the other hand, treat the avoidance of error as more imperative, and let truth take its chance. Clifford, in the instructive passage which I have quoted, exhorts us to the latter course. Believe nothing, he tells us, keep your mind in suspense forever, rather than by closing it on insufficient evidence incur the awful risk of believing lies. You, on the other hand, may think that the risk of being in error is a very small matter when compared with the blessings of real knowledge, and be ready to be duped many times in your investigation rather than postpone indefinitely the chance of guessing true. I myself find it impossible to go with Clifford. We must remember that these feelings of our duty about either truth or error are in any case only expressions of our passional life. Biologically considered, our minds are as ready to grind out falsehood as veracity, and he who says, "Better go without belief forever than believe a lie!" merely shows his own preponderant private horror of becoming a dupe. He may be critical of many of his desires and fears, but this fear he slavishly obeys. He cannot imagine any one questioning its binding force. For my own part, I have also a horror of being duped; but I can believe that worse things than being duped may happen to a man in this world: so Clifford's exhortation has to my ears a thoroughly fantastic sound. It is like a general informing his soldiers that it is better to keep out of battle forever than to risk a single wound. Not so are victories either over enemies or over nature gained. Our errors are surely not such awfully solemn things. In a world where we are so certain to incur them in spite of all our caution, a certain lightness of heart seems healthier than this excessive nervousness on their behalf. At any rate, it seems the fittest thing for the empiricist philosopher.

VIII

And now, after all this introduction, let us go straight at our question. I have said, and now repeat it, that not only as a matter of fact do we find our passional nature influencing us in our opinions, but that there are some options between opinions in which this influence must be regarded both as an inevitable and as a lawful determinant of our choice.

I fear here that some of you my hearers will begin to scent danger, and lend an inhospitable ear. Two first steps of passion you have indeed had to admit as necessary—we must think so as to avoid dupery, and we must think so as to gain truth; but the surest path to those ideal consummations, you will probably consider, is from now onwards to take no further passional step.

Well, of course, I agree as far as the facts will allow. Wherever the option between losing truth and gaining it is not momentous, we can throw the chance of *gaining truth* away, and at any rate save ourselves from any chance of *believing falsehood,* by not making up our minds at all till objective evidence has come. In scientific questions, this is almost always the case; and even in human affairs in general, the need of acting is seldom so urgent that a false belief to act on is better than no belief at all. Law courts, indeed, have to decide on the best evidence attainable for the moment, because a judge's duty is to make law as well as to ascertain it, and (as a learned judge once said to me) few cases are worth spending much time over: the great thing is to have them decided on *any* acceptable principle, and got out of the way. But in our dealings with objective nature we obviously are recorders, not makers, of the truth; and decisions for the mere sake of deciding promptly and getting on to the next business would be wholly out of place. Throughout the breadth of physical nature facts are what they are quite independently of us, and seldom is there any such hurry about them that the risks of being duped by believing a premature theory need be faced. The questions here are always trivial options, the hypotheses are hardly living (at any rate not living for us spectators), the choice between believing truth or falsehood is seldom forced. The attitude of sceptical balance is therefore the absolutely wise one if we would escape mistakes. What difference, indeed, does it make to most of us whether we have or have not a theory of the Röntgen rays, whether we believe or not in mind-stuff, or have a conviction about the causality of conscious states? It makes no difference. Such options are not forced on us. On every account it is better not to make them, but still keep weighing reasons *pro et contra* with an indifferent hand.

I speak, of course, here of the purely judging mind. For purposes of discovery such indifference is to be less highly recommended, and science would be far less advanced than she is if the passionate desires of individuals to get their own faiths confirmed had been kept out of the game. See for example the sagacity which Spencer and Weismann now display. On the other hand, if you want an absolute duffer in an investigation, you must, after all, take the man who has no interest whatever in its results: he is the warranted incapable, the positive fool. The most useful investigator, because the most sensitive observer, is always he whose eager interest in one side of the question is balanced by an equally keen nervousness lest he become deceived.[2] Science has organized this nervousness into a regular *technique,* her so-called method of verification; and she has fallen so deeply in love with the method that one may even say she has ceased to care for truth by itself at all. It is only truth as technically verified that interests her. The truth of truths might come in merely affirmative form, and she would decline to touch it. Such truth as that, she might repeat with Clifford, would be stolen in defiance of her duty to mankind. Human passions, however, are stronger than technical rules. "Le cœur a ses raisons," as Pascal says, "que la raison ne connaît pas;" and however indifferent to all but the bare rules of the game the umpire, the abstract intellect, may be, the concrete players who furnish him the materials to judge of are usually, each one of them, in love with some pet "live hypothesis" of his own. Let us agree, however, that wherever there is no forced option, the dispassionately judicial intellect with no pet hypothesis, saving us, as it does, from dupery at any rate, ought to be our ideal.

The question next arises: Are there not somewhere forced options in our speculative questions, and can we (as men who may be interested at least as much in positively gaining truth as in merely escaping dupery) always wait with impunity till the coercive evidence shall have arrived? It seems *a priori* improbable that the truth should be so nicely adjusted to our needs and powers as that. In the great boarding-house of nature, the cakes and the butter and the syrup seldom come out so even and leave the plates so clean. Indeed, we should view them with scientific suspicion if they did.

[2] Compare Wilfrid Ward's Essay, "The Wish to Believe," in his *Witness to the Unseen,* Macmillan & Co., 1893.

IX

Moral questions immediately present themselves as questions whose solution cannot wait for sensible proof. A moral question is a question not of what sensibly exists, but of what is good, or would be good if it did exist. Science can tell us what exists; but to compare the *worths,* both of what exists and of what does not exist, we must consult not science, but what Pascal calls our heart. Science herself consults her heart when she lays it down that the infinite ascertainment of fact and correction of false belief are the supreme goods for man. Challenge the statement, and science can only repeat it oracularly, or else prove it by showing that such ascertainment and correction bring man all sorts of other goods which man's heart in turn declares. The question of having moral beliefs at all or not having them is decided by our will. Are our moral preferences true or false, or are they only odd biological phenomena, making things good or bad for *us,* but in themselves indifferent? How can your pure intellect decide? If your heart does not *want* a world of moral reality, your head will assuredly never make you believe in one. Mephistophelian scepticism, indeed, will satisfy the head's play-instincts much better than any rigorous idealism can. Some men (even at the student age) are so naturally cool-hearted that the moralistic hypothesis never has for them any pungent life, and in their supercilious presence the hot young moralist always feels strangely ill at ease. The appearance of knowingness is on their side, of *naïveté* and gullibility on his. Yet, in the inarticulate heart of him, he clings to it that he is not a dupe, and that there is a realm in which (as Emerson says) all their wit and intellectual superiority is no better than the cunning of a fox. Moral scepticism can no more be refuted or proved by logic than intellectual scepticism can. When we stick to it that there *is* truth (be it of either kind), we do so with our whole nature, and resolve to stand or fall by the results. The sceptic with his whole nature adopts the doubting attitude; but which of us is the wiser, Omniscience only knows.

Turn now from these wide questions of good to a certain class of questions of fact, questions concerning personal relations, states of mind between one man and another. *Do you like me or not?*—

for example. Whether you do or not depends, in countless instances, on whether I meet you half-way, am willing to assume that you must like me, and show you trust and expectation. The previous faith on my part in your liking's existence is in such cases what makes your liking come. But if I stand aloof, and refuse to budge an inch until I have objective evidence, until you shall have done something apt, as the absolutists say, *ad extorquendum assensum meum,* ten to one your liking never comes. How many women's hearts are vanquished by the mere sanguine insistence of some man that they *must* love him! he will not consent to the hypothesis that they cannot. The desire for a certain kind of truth here brings about that special truth's existence; and so it is in innumerable cases of other sorts. Who gains promotions, boons, appointments, but the man in whose life they are seen to play the part of live hypotheses, who discounts them, sacrifices other things for their sake before they have come, and takes risks for them in advance? His faith acts on the powers above him as a claim, and creates its own verification.

A social organism of any sort whatever, large or small, is what it is because each member proceeds to his own duty with a trust that the other members will simultaneously do theirs. Wherever a desired result is achieved by the cooperation of many independent persons, its existence as a fact is a pure consequence of the pre-cursive faith in one another of those immediately concerned. A government, an army, a commercial system, a ship, a college, an athletic team, all exist on this condition, without which not only is nothing achieved, but nothing is even attempted. A whole train of passengers (individually brave enough) will be looted by a few highwaymen, simply because the latter can count on one another, while each passenger fears that if he makes a movement of re-sistance, he will be shot before any one else backs him up. If we believed that the whole car-full would rise at once with us, we should each severally rise, and train-robbing would never even be attempted. There are, then, cases where a fact cannot come at all unless a preliminary faith exists in its coming. *And where faith in a fact can help create the fact,* that would be an insane logic which should say that faith running ahead of scientific evidence is the "lowest kind of immorality" into which a thinking being can fall. Yet such is the logic by which our scientific absolutists pretend to regulate our lives!

X

In truths dependent on our personal action, then, faith based on desire is certainly a lawful and possibly an indispensable thing.

But now, it will be said, these are all childish human cases, and have nothing to do with great cosmical matters, like the question of religious faith. Let us then pass on to that. Religions differ so much in their accidents that in discussing the religious question we must make it very generic and broad. What then do we now mean by the religious hypothesis? Science says things are; morality says some things are better than other things; and religion says essentially two things.

First, she says that the best things are the more eternal things, the overlapping things, the things in the universe that throw the last stone, so to speak, and say the final word. "Perfection is eternal" —this phrase of Charles Secrétan seems a good way of putting this first affirmation of religion, an affirmation which obviously cannot yet be verified scientifically at all.

The second affirmation of religion is that we are better off even now if we believe her first affirmation to be true.

Now, let us consider what the logical elements of this situation are *in case the religious hypothesis in both its branches be really true.* (Of course, we must admit that possibility at the outset. If we are to discuss the question at all, it must involve a living option. If for any of you religion be a hypothesis that cannot, by any living possibility be true, then you need go no farther. I speak to the "saving remnant" alone.) So proceeding, we see, first, that religion offers itself as a *momentous* option. We are supposed to gain, even now, by our belief, and to lose by our nonbelief, a certain vital good. Secondly, religion is a *forced* option, so far as that good goes. We cannot escape the issue by remaining sceptical and waiting for more light, because, although we do avoid error in that way *if religion be untrue,* we lose the good, *if it be true,* just as certainly as if we positively chose to disbelieve. It is as if a man should hesitate indefinitely to ask a certain woman to marry him because he was not perfectly sure that she would prove an angel after he brought her home. Would he not cut himself off from that particular angel-possibility as decisively as if he went and married some one else? Scepticism, then, is not avoidance of option; it is option of a certain particular kind of risk. *Better risk loss of truth than chance of error*—that is your faith-vetoer's exact position. He is actively playing his stake as much as the believer is; he is backing the field against the religious hypothesis, just as the believer is backing the religious hypothesis against the field. To preach scepticism to us as a duty until "sufficient evidence" for religion be found, is tantamount therefore to telling us, when in presence of the religious hypothesis, that to yield to our fear of its being error is wiser and better than to yield to our hope that it may be true. It is not intellect against all passions, then; it is only intellect with one passion laying down its law. And by what, forsooth, is the supreme wisdom of this passion warranted? Dupery for dupery, what proof is there that dupery through hope is so much worse than dupery through fear? I, for one, can see no proof; and I simply refuse obedience to the scientist's command to imitate his kind of option, in a case where my own stake is important enough to give me the right to choose my own form of risk. If religion be true and the evidence for it be still insufficient, I do not wish, by putting your extinguisher upon my nature (which feels to me as if it had after all some business in this matter), to forfeit my sole chance in life of getting upon the winning side—that chance depending, of course, on my willingness to run the risk of acting as if my passional need of taking the world religiously might be prophetic and right.

All this is on the supposition that it really may be prophetic and right, and that, even to us who are discussing the matter, religion is a live hypothesis which may be true. Now, to most of us religion comes in a still further way that makes a veto on our active faith even more illogical. The more perfect and more eternal aspect of the universe is represented in our religions as having personal form. The universe is no longer a mere *It* to us, but a

Thou, if we are religious; and any relation that may be possible from person to person might be possible here. For instance, although in one sense we are passive portions of the universe, in another we show a curious autonomy, as if we were small active centres on our own account. We feel, too, as if the appeal of religion to us were made to our own active good will, as if evidence might be forever withheld from us unless we met the hypothesis half-way. To take a trivial illustration: just as a man who in a company of gentlemen made no advances, asked a warrant for every concession, and believed no one's word without proof, would cut himself off by such churlishness from all the social rewards that a more trusting spirit would earn—so here, one who should shut himself up in snarling logicality and try to make the gods extort his recognition willy-nilly, or not get it at all, might cut himself off forever from his only opportunity of making the gods' acquaintance. This feeling, forced on us we know not whence, that by obstinately believing that there are gods (although not to do so would be so easy both for our logic and our life) we are doing the universe the deepest service we can, seems part of the living essence of the religious hypothesis. If the hypothesis *were* true in all its parts, including this one, then pure intellectualism, with its veto on our making willing advances, would be an absurdity; and some participation of our sympathetic nature would be logically required. I, therefore, for one, cannot see my way to accepting the agnostic rules for truth-seeking, or wilfully agree to keep my willing nature out of the game. I cannot do so for this plain reason, that *a rule of thinking which would absolutely prevent me from acknowledging certain kinds of truth if those kinds of truth were really there, would be an irrational rule.* That for me is the long and short of the formal logic of the situation, no matter what the kinds of truth might materially be.

I confess I do not see how this logic can be escaped. But sad experience makes me fear that some of you may still shrink from radically saying with me, *in abstracto,* that we have the right to believe at our own risk any hypothesis that is live enough to tempt our will. I suspect, however, that if this is so, it is because you have got away from the abstract logical point of view altogether, and are thinking (perhaps without realizing it) of some particular religious hypothesis which for you is dead. The freedom to "believe what we will" you apply to the case of some patent superstition; and the faith you think of is the faith defined by the schoolboy when he said, "Faith is when you believe something that you know ain't true." I can only repeat that this is misapprehension. *In concreto,* the freedom to believe can only cover living options which the intellect of the individual cannot by itself resolve; and living options never seem absurdities to him who has them to consider. When I look at the religious question as it really puts itself to concrete men, and when I think of all the possibilities which both practically and theoretically it involves, then this command that we shall put a stopper on our heart, instincts, and courage, and *wait*—acting of course meanwhile more or less as if religion were *not* true[3]—till doomsday, or till such time as our intellect and senses working together may have raked in evidence enough—this command, I say, seems to me the queerest idol ever manufactured in the philosophic cave. Were we scholastic absolutists, there might be more excuse. If we had an infallible intellect with its objective certitudes, we might feel ourselves disloyal to such a perfect organ of knowledge in not trusting to it exclusively, in not waiting for its releasing word. But if we are empiricists, if we believe that no bell in us tolls to let us know for certain when truth is in our grasp, then it seems a piece of idle fantasticality to preach so solemnly our duty of waiting for the bell. Indeed we *may* wait if we will—I hope you do not think that I am denying that— but if we do so, we do so at our peril as much as if we believed. In either case we *act,* taking our life in our hands. No one of us

---

[3] Since belief is measured by action, he who forbids us to believe religion to be true, necessarily also forbids us to act as we should if we did believe it to be true. The whole defence of religious faith hinges upon action. If the action required or inspired by the religious hypothesis is in no way different from that dictated by the naturalistic hypothesis, then religious faith is a pure superfluity, better pruned away, and controversy about its legitimacy is a piece of idle trifling, unworthy of serious minds. I myself believe, of course, that the religious hypothesis gives to the world an expression which specifically determines our reactions, and makes them in a large part unlike what they might be on a purely naturalistic scheme of belief.

ought to issue vetoes to the other, nor should we bandy words of abuse. We ought, on the contrary, delicately and profoundly to respect one another's mental freedom: then only shall we bring about the intellectual republic; then only shall we have that spirit of inner tolerance without which all our outer tolerance is soulless, and which is empiricism's glory; then only shall we live and let live, in speculative as well as in practical things.

I began by a reference to Fitz James Stephen; let me end by a quotation from him. "What do you think of yourself? What do you think of the world? . . . These are questions with which all must deal as it seems good to them. They are riddles of the Sphinx, and in some way or other we must deal with them. . . . In all important transactions of life we have to take a leap in the dark. . . . If we decide to leave the riddles unanswered, that is a choice; if we waver in our answer, that, too, is a choice: but whatever choice we make, we make it at our peril. If a man chooses to turn his back altogether on God and the future, no one can prevent him; no one can show beyond reasonable doubt that he is mistaken. If a man thinks otherwise and acts as he thinks, I do not see that any one can prove that *he* is mistaken. Each must act as he thinks best; and if he is wrong, so much the worse for him. We stand on a mountain pass in the midst of whirling snow and blinding mist, through which we get glimpses now and then of paths which may be deceptive. If we stand still we shall be frozen to death. If we take the wrong road we shall be dashed to pieces. We do not certainly know whether there is any right one. What must we do? 'Be strong and of a good courage.' Act for the best, hope for the best, and take what comes. . . . If death ends all, we cannot meet death better." [4]

[4] *Liberty, Equality, Fraternity*, p. 353, 2d edition. London, 1874.

SØREN KIERKEGAARD

Faith as Passionate
Commitment

Søren Kierkegaard (1813–1855) was a Dane, and his work is one
of the main sources of the existentialist tradition in philosophy.
Some of his main works are *Concluding Unscientific Postscript,
Philosophical Fragments* and *Either-Or.*

In an attempt to make clear the difference of way that exists between an objective and a subjective reflection, I shall now proceed
to show how a subjective reflection makes its way inwardly in inwardness. Inwardness in an existing subject culminates in passion;
corresponding to passion in the subject the truth becomes a paradox; and the fact that the truth becomes a paradox is rooted
precisely in its having a relationship to an existing subject. Thus
the one corresponds to the other. By forgetting that one is an existing subject, passion goes by the board and the truth is no longer
a paradox; the knowing subject becomes a fantastic entity rather
than a human being, and the truth becomes a fantastic object for
the knowledge of this fantastic entity.

*When the question of truth is raised in an objective manner,
reflection is directed objectively to the truth, as an object to which*

* From S. Kierkegaard, *Concluding Unscientific Postscript,* tr. by D. Swenson.
Reprinted by permission of Princeton University Press and the American Scan-
dinavian Foundation.

184

the knower is related. Reflection is not focussed upon the relation-
ship, however, but upon the question of whether it is the truth
to which the knower is related. If only the object to which he is
related is the truth, the subject is accounted to be in the truth.
When the question of the truth is raised subjectively, reflection is
directed subjectively to the nature of the individual's relationship;
if only the mode of this relationship is in the truth, the individual is
in the truth even if he should happen to be thus related to what is
not true.[1] Let us take as an example the knowledge of God. Objectively, reflection is directed to the problem of whether this object
is the true God; subjectively, reflection is directed to the question
whether the individual is related to a something *in such a manner*
that his relationship is in truth a God-relationship. On which side
is the truth now to be found? Ah, may we not here resort to a
mediation, and say: It is on neither side, but in the mediation of
both? Excellently well said, provided we might have it explained
how an existing individual manages to be in a state of mediation.
For to be in a state of mediation is to be finished, while to exist
is to become. Nor can an existing individual be in two places at
the same time—he cannot be an identity of subject and object.
When he is nearest to being in two places at the same time he is
in passion; but passion is momentary, and passion is also the highest expression of subjectivity.

The existing individual who chooses to pursue the objective
way enters upon the entire approximation-process by which it is
proposed to bring God to light objectively. But this is in all
eternity impossible, because God is a subject, and therefore exists
only for subjectivity in inwardness. The existing individual who
chooses the subjective way apprehends instantly the entire dialectical difficulty involved in having to use some time, perhaps a
long time, in finding God objectively; and he feels this dialectical
difficulty in all its painfulness, because every moment is wasted in
which he does not have God.[2] That very instant he has God, not

[1] The reader will observe that the question here is about essential truth, or
about the truth which is essentially related to existence, and that it is precisely
for the sake of clarifying it as inwardness or as subjectivity that this contrast
is drawn.

by virtue of any objective deliberation, but by virtue of the infinite passion of inwardness. The objective inquirer, on the other hand, is not embarrassed by such dialectical difficulties as are involved in devoting an entire period of investigation to finding God —since it is possible that the inquirer may die tomorrow; and if he lives he can scarcely regard God as something to be taken along if convenient, since God is precisely that which one takes *a tout prix,* which in the understanding of passion constitutes the true inward relationship to God.

It is at this point, so difficult dialectically, that the way swings off for everyone who knows what it means to think, and to think existentially; which is something very different from sitting at a desk and writing about what one has never done, something very different from writing *de omnibus dubitandum* and at the same time being as credulous existentially as the most sensuous of men. Here is where the way swings off, and the change is marked by the fact that while objective knowledge rambles comfortably on by way of the long road of approximation without being impelled by the urge of passion, subjective knowledge counts every delay a deadly peril, and the decision so infinitely important and so instantly pressing that it is as if the opportunity had already passed.

Now when the problem is to reckon up on which side there is most truth, whether on the side of one who seeks the true God objectively, and pursues the approximate truth of the God-idea; or on the side of one who, driven by the infinite passion of his need of God, feels an infinite concern for his own relationship to God in truth (and to be at one and the same time on both sides equally, is as we have noted not possible for an existing individual, but is merely the happy delusion of an imaginary I-am-I): the answer cannot be in doubt for anyone who has not been demoralized with

[2] In this manner God certainly becomes a postulate, but not in the otiose manner in which this word is commonly understood. It becomes clear rather that the only way in which an existing individual comes into relation with God, is when the dialectical contradiction brings his passion to the point of despair, and helps him to embrace God with the "category of despair" (faith). Then the postulate is so far from being arbitrary that it is precisely a life-necessity. It is then not so much that God is a postulate, as that the existing individual's postulation of God is a necessity.

the aid of science. If one who lives in the midst of Christendom goes up to the house of God, the house of the true God, with the true conception of God in his knowledge, and prays, but prays in a false spirit; and one who lives in an idolatrous community prays with the entire passion of the infinite, although his eyes rest upon the image of an idol: where is there most truth? The one prays in truth to God though he worships an idol; the other prays falsely to the true God, and hence worships in fact an idol.

When one man investigates objectively the problem of immortality, and another embraces an uncertainty with the passion of the infinite: where is there most truth, and who has the greater certainty? The one has entered upon a never-ending approximation, for the certainty of immortality lies precisely in the subjectivity of the individual; the other is immortal, and fights for his immortality by struggling with the uncertainty. Let us consider Socrates. Nowadays everyone dabbles in a few proofs; some have several such proofs, others fewer. But Socrates! He puts the question objectively in a problematic manner: *if* there is an immortality. He must therefore be accounted a doubter in comparison with one of our modern thinkers with the three proofs? By no means. On this "if" he risks his entire life, he has the courage to meet death, and he has the passion of the infinite so determined the pattern of his life that it must be found acceptable—*if* there is an immortality. Is any better proof capable of being given for the immortality of the soul? But those who have the three proofs do not at all determine their lives in conformity therewith; if there is an immortality it must feel disgust over their manner of life: can any better refutation be given of the three proofs? The bit of uncertainty that Socrates had, helped him because he himself contributed the passion of the infinite; the three proofs that the others have do not profit them at all, because they are dead to spirit and enthusiasm, and their three proofs, in lieu of proving anything else, prove just this. A young girl may enjoy all the sweetness of love on the basis of what is merely a weak hope that she is beloved, because she rests everything on this weak hope; but many a wedded matron more than once subjected to the strongest expressions of love, has in so far indeed had proofs, but strangely enough has not enjoyed *quod doesn't feel she can draw QE!)*

erat demonstrandum. The Socratic ignorance, which Socrates held fast with the entire passion of his inwardness, was thus an expression for the principle that the eternal truth is related to an existing individual, and that this truth must therefore be a paradox for him as long as he exists; and yet it is possible that there was more truth in the Socratic ignorance as it was in him, than in the entire objective truth of the System, which flirts with what the times demand and accommodates itself to *Privatdocents.*

⌐*The objective accent falls on WHAT is said, the subjective accent on HOW it is said.*⌐ This distinction holds even in the aesthetic realm, and receives definite expression in the principle that what is in itself true may in the mouth of such and such a person become untrue. In these times this distinction is particularly worthy of notice, for if we wish to express in a single sentence the difference between ancient times and our own, we should doubtless have to say: "In ancient times only an individual here and there knew the truth; now all know it, except that the inwardness of its appropriation stands in an inverse relationship to the extent of its dissemination.[3] Aesthetically the contradiction that truth becomes untruth in this or that person's mouth, is best construed comically: In the ethico-religious sphere, accent is again on the "how." But this is not to be understood as referring to demeanor, expression, or the like; rather it refers to the relationship sustained by the existing individual, in his own existence, to the content of his utter-

---

[3] *Stages on Life's Way,* Note on p. 426. Though ordinarily not wishing an expression of opinion on the part of reviewers, I might at this point almost desire it, provided such opinions, so far from flattering me, amounted to an assertion of the daring truth that what I say is something that everybody knows, even every child, and that the cultured know infinitely much better. If it only stands fast that everyone knows it, my standpoint is in order, and I shall doubtless make shift to manage with the unity of the comic and the tragic. If there were anyone who did not know it I might perhaps be in danger of being dislodged from my position of equilibrium by the thought that I might be in a position to communicate to someone the needful preliminary knowledge. It is just this which engages my interest so much, this that the cultured are accustomed to say: that everyone knows what the highest is. This was not the case in paganism, nor in Judaism, nor in the seventeen centuries of Christianity. Hail to the nineteenth century! Everyone knows it. What progress has been made since the time when only a few knew it. To make up for this, perhaps, we must assume that no one nowadays does it.

ance. Objectively the interest is focussed merely on the thought-content, subjectively on the inwardness. At its maximum this inward "how" is the passion of the infinite, and the passion of the infinite is the truth. But the passion of the infinite is precisely subjectivity, and thus subjectivity becomes the truth. Objectively there is no infinite decisiveness, and hence it is objectively in order to annul the difference between good and evil, together with the principle of contradiction, and therewith also the infinite difference between the true and the false. Only in subjectivity is there decisiveness, to seek objectivity is to be in error. It is the passion of the infinite that is the decisive factor and not its content, for its content is precisely itself. In this manner subjectivity and the subjective "how" constitute the truth.

But the "how" which is thus subjectively accentuated precisely because the subject is an existing individual, is also subject to a dialectic with respect to time. In the passionate moment of decision, where the road swings away from objective knowledge, it seems as if the infinite decision were thereby realized. But in the same moment the existing individual finds himself in the temporal order, and the subjective "how" is transformed into a striving, a striving which receives indeed its impulse and a repeated renewal from the decisive passion of the infinite, but is nevertheless a striving.

When subjectivity is the truth, the conceptual determination of the truth must include an expression for the antithesis to objectivity, a memento of the fork in the road where the way swings off; this expression will at the same time serve as an indication of the tension of the subjective inwardness. Here is such a definition of truth: *An objective uncertainty held fast in an appropriation-process of the most passionate inwardness is the truth,* the highest truth attainable for an *existing* individual. At the point where the way swings off (and where this is cannot be specified objectively, since it is a matter of subjectivity), there objective knowledge is placed in abeyance. Thus the subject merely has, objectively, the uncertainty; but it is this which precisely increases the tension of that infinite passion which constitutes his inwardness. The truth is precisely the venture which chooses an objective uncertainty with the passion of the infinite. I contemplate the order of nature in the hope of finding God, and I see omnipotence and wisdom; but I also see much else that disturbs my mind and excites anxiety. The sum of all this is an objective uncertainty. But it is for this very reason that the inwardness becomes as intense as it is, for it embraces this objective uncertainty with the entire passion of the infinite. In the case of a mathematical proposition the objectivity is given, but for this reason the truth of such a proposition is also an indifferent truth.

But the above definition of truth is an equivalent expression for faith. Without risk there is no faith. Faith is precisely the contradiction between the infinite passion of the individual's inwardness and the objective uncertainty. If I am capable of grasping God objectively, I do not believe, but precisely because I cannot do this I must believe. If I wish to preserve myself in faith I must constantly be intent upon holding fast the objective uncertainty, so as to remain out upon the deep, over seventy thousand fathoms of water, still preserving my faith.

In the principle that subjectivity, inwardness, is the truth, there is comprehended the Socratic wisdom, whose everlasting merit it was to have become aware of the essential significance of existence, of the fact that the knower is an existing individual. For this reason Socrates was in the truth by virtue of his ignorance, in the highest sense in which this was possible within paganism. To attain to an understanding of this, to comprehend that the misfortune of speculative philosophy is again and again to have forgotten that the knower is an existing individual, is in our objective age difficult enough. . . .

LUDWIG A. FEUERBACH

God as a Projection

Ludwig A. Feuerbach (1804–1872) was a leading German religious philosopher. His main work is *The Essence of Christianity*.

THE ESSENCE OF RELIGION CONSIDERED GENERALLY

What we have hitherto been maintaining generally, even with regard to sensational impressions, of the relation between subject and object, applies especially to the relation between the subject and the religious object.

In the perceptions of the senses consciousness of the object is distinguishable from consciousness of self; but in religion, consciousness of the object and self-consciousness coincide. The object of the senses is out of man, the religious object is within him, and therefore as little forsakes him as his self-consciousness or his conscience; it is the intimate, the closest object. "God," says Augustine, for example, "is nearer, more related to us, and therefore more easily known by us, than sensible, corporeal things." [1] The object of the senses is in itself indifferent—independent of the disposition or of the judgment; but the object of religion is a selected object; the most excellent, the first, the supreme being; it essentially presup-

* From L. Feuerbach, *The Essence of Christianity,* tr. by M. Evans.
[1] *De Genesi ad litteram,* l. v. c. 16.

191

poses a critical judgment, a discrimination between the divine and the nondivine, between that which is worthy of adoration and that which is not worthy.[2] And here may be applied, without any limitation, the proposition: the object of any subject is nothing else than the subject's own nature taken objectively. (Such as are a man's thoughts and dispositions, such is his God;) so much worth as a man has, so much and no more has his God. Consciousness of God is self-consciousness, knowledge of God is self-knowledge. By his God thou knowest the man, and by the man his God; the two are identical. Whatever is God to a man, that is his heart and soul; and conversely, God is the manifested inward nature, the expressed self of a man—religion the solemn unveiling of a man's hidden treasures, the revelation of his intimate thoughts, the open confession of his love-secrets.

But when religion—consciousness of God—is designated as the self-consciousness of man, this is not to be understood as affirming that the religious man is directly aware of this identity; for, on the contrary, ignorance of it is fundamental to the peculiar nature of religion. To preclude this misconception, it is better to say, religion is man's earliest and also indirect form of self-knowledge. Hence, religion everywhere precedes philosophy, as in the history of the race, so also in that of the individual. Man first of all sees his nature as if *out of* himself, before he finds it in himself. His own nature is in the first instance contemplated by him as that of another being. Religion is the childlike condition of humanity; but the child sees his nature—man—out of himself; in childhood a man is an object to himself, under the form of another man. Hence the historical progress of religion consists in this: that what by an earlier religion was regarded as objective, is now recognised as subjective; that is, what was formerly contemplated and worshipped as God is now perceived to be something *human*. What was at first religion becomes at a later period idolatry; man is seen to have adored his own nature. Man has given objectivity to himself, but has not recognised the object as his own nature: a later religion takes this forward step; every advance in religion is therefore

[2] *Unusquisque vestrum non cogitat*, prius *se debere Deum* nosse, *quam* colere. —M. *Minucii Felicis Octavianus*, c. 24.

a deeper self-knowledge. But every particular religion, while it pronounces its predecessors idolatrous, excepts itself—and necessarily so, otherwise it would no longer be religion—from the fate, the common nature of all religions: it imputes only to other religions what is the fault, if fault it be, of religion in general. Because it has a different object, a different tenour, because it has transcended the ideas of preceding religions, it erroneously supposes itself exalted above the necessary eternal laws which constitute the essence of religion—it fancies its object, its ideas, to be superhuman. But the essence of religion, thus hidden from the religious, is evident to the thinker, by whom religion is viewed objectively, which it cannot be by its votaries. And it is our task to show that the antithesis of divine and human is altogether illusory, that it is nothing else than the antithesis between the human nature in general, and the human individual: that, consequently, the object and contents of the Christian religion are altogether human.

Religion, at least the Christian, is the relation of man to himself, or more correctly to his own nature (*i.e.*, his subjective nature);[3] but a relation to it, viewed as a nature apart from his own. The divine being is nothing else than the human being, or, rather the human nature purified, freed from the limits of the individual man, made objective—that is, contemplated and revered as another, a distinct being. All the attributes of the divine nature are, therefore, attributes of the human nature.[4]

. . . .

GOD AS A BEING OF THE UNDERSTANDING

Religion is the disuniting of man from himself: he sets God before him as the antithesis of himself. God is not what man is—man is

[3] The meaning of this parenthetic limitation will be clear in the sequel.
[4] *Les perfections de Dieu sont celles de nos âmes, mais il les possede sans bornes—il y a en nous quelque puissance, quelque connaissance, quelque bonté, mais elles sont toutes entières en Dieu.*—Leibnitz, (*Théod. Preface.*) *Nihil in anima esse putemus eximium, quod non etiam divinæ naturæ proprium sit— Quidquid a Deo alienum extra definitionem animæ.*—S. Gregorius Nyss. *Est ergo, ut videtur, disciplinarum omnium pulcherrima et maxima se ipsum nosse; si quis enim se ipsum norit, Deum cognoscet.*—Clemens Alex. (*Pæd.* 1. iii. c. 1.)

not what God is. God is the infinite, man the finite being; God is perfect, man imperfect; God eternal, man temporal; God almighty, man weak; God holy, man sinful. God and man are extremes: God is the absolutely positive, the sum of all realities; man the absolutely negative, comprehending all negations.

But in religion man contemplates his own latent nature. Hence it must be shown that this antithesis, this differencing of God and man, with which religion begins, is a differencing of man with his own nature.

The inherent necessity of this proof is at once apparent from this—that if the divine nature, which is the object of religion, were really different from the nature of man, a division, a disunion could not take place. If God is really a different being from myself, why should his perfection trouble me? Disunion exists only between beings who are at variance, but who ought to be one, who can be one, and who consequently in nature, in truth, are one. On this general ground, then, the nature with which man feels himself in disunion, must be inborn, immanent in himself, but at the same time it must be of a different character from that nature or power which gives him the feeling, the consciousness of reconciliation, of union with God, or, what is the same thing, with himself.

This nature is nothing else than the intelligence—the reason or the understanding. God as the antithesis of man, as a being not human, that is, not personally human, is the objective nature of the understanding. The pure, perfect divine nature is the self-consciousness of the understanding, the consciousness which the understanding has of its own perfection. The understanding knows nothing of the sufferings of the heart; it has no desires, no passions, no wants, and for that reason, no deficiencies and weaknesses, as the heart has. Men in whom the intellect predominates, who with one-sided but all the more characteristic definiteness, embody and personify for us the nature of the understanding, are free from the anguish of the heart, from the passions, the excesses of the man who has strong emotions; they are not passionately interested in any finite, that is, particular object; they do not give themselves in pledge; they are free. "To want nothing, and by this freedom from wants to become like the immortal Gods"; "not to subject ourselves to things but things to us"; "all is vanity"; these and similar sayings are the mottoes of the men who are governed by abstract understanding. The understanding is that part of our nature which is neutral, impassible, not to be bribed, not subject to illusions—the pure, passionless light of the intelligence. It is the categorical, impartial consciousness of the fact as fact, because it is itself of an objective nature. It is the consciousness of the uncontradictory, because it is itself the uncontradictory unity, the source of logical identity. It is the consciousness of law, necessity, rule, measure, because it is itself the activity of law, the necessity of the nature of things under the form of spontaneous activity, the rule of rules, the absolute measure, the measure of measures. Only by the understanding can man judge and act in contradiction with his dearest human, that is, personal feelings, when the God of the understanding—law, necessity, right—commands it. The father who as a judge condemns his own son to death because he knows him to be guilty, can do this only as a rational not as an emotional being. The understanding shews us the faults and weaknesses even of our beloved ones; it shews us even our own. It is for this reason that it so often throws us into painful collision with ourselves, with our own hearts. We do not like to give reason the upper hand: we are too tender to ourselves to carry out the true, but hard, relentless verdict of the understanding. The understanding is the power which has relation to species: the heart represents particular circumstances, individuals—the understanding, general circumstances, universals; it is the superhuman, that is, the impersonal power in man. Only by and in the understanding has man the power of abstraction from himself, from his subjective being—of exalting himself to general ideas and relations, of distinguishing the object from the impressions which it produces on his feelings, of regarding it in and by itself without reference to human personality. Philosophy, mathematics, astronomy, physics, in short, science in general, is the practical proof, because it is the product, of this truly infinite and divine activity. Religious anthropomorphisms, therefore, are in contradiction with the understanding; it repudiates their application to God; it denies them. But this God, free from

196 / LUDWIG A. FEUERBACH

anthropomorphisms, impartial, passionless, is nothing else than the nature of the understanding itself regarded as objective.

God as God, that is, as a being not finite, not human, not materially conditioned, not phenomenal, is only an object of thought. He is the incorporeal, formless, incomprehensible—the abstract, negative being: he is known, that is, becomes an object, only by abstraction and negation (*via negationis*). Why? Because he is nothing but the objective nature of the thinking power, or in general, of the power or activity, name it what you will, whereby man is conscious of reason, of mind, of intelligence. There is no other spirit, that is (for the idea of spirit is simply the idea of thought, of intelligence, of understanding, every other spirit being a spectre of the imagination), no other intelligence which man can believe in or conceive, than that intelligence which enlightens him, which is active in him. He can do nothing more than separate the intelligence from the limitations of his own individuality. The "infinite spirit," in distinction from the finite, is therefore nothing else than the intelligence disengaged from the limits of individuality and corporeality—for individuality and corporeality are inseparable —intelligence posited in and by itself. God, said the schoolmen, the Christian fathers, and long before them the heathen philosophers—God is immaterial essence, intelligence, spirit, pure understanding. Of God as God, no image can be made; but canst thou frame an image of mind? Has mind a form? Is not its activity the most inexplicable, the most incapable of representation? God is incomprehensible; but knowest thou the nature of the intelligence? Hast thou searched out the mysterious operation of thought, the hidden nature of self-consciousness? It not self-consciousness the enigma of enigmas? Did not the old mystics, schoolmen, and fathers, long ago compare the incomprehensibility of the divine nature with that of the human intelligence, and thus, in truth, identify the nature of God with the nature of man? [5] God as God—as a purely

[5] Augustine, in his work *Contra Academicos*, which he wrote when he was still in some measure a heathen, says (l. iii. c. 12), that the highest good of man consists in the mind, or in the reason. On the other hand, in his *Libr. Retractationum*, which he wrote as a distinguished Christian and theologian, he revises (l. i. c. 1) this declaration as follows: *Verius dixissem in Deo. Ipso enim*

thinkable being, an object of the intellect—is thus nothing else than the reason in its utmost intensification become objective to itself. It is asked what is the understanding or the reason? The answer is found in the idea of God. Everything must express itself, reveal itself, make itself objective, affirm itself. God is the reason expressing, affirming itself as the highest existence. To the imagination, the reason is the revelation of God; but to the reason, God is the revelation of the reason; since what reason is, what it can do, is first made objective in God. God is a need of the intelligence, a necessary thought—the highest degree of the thinking power. "The reason cannot rest in sensuous things"; it can find contentment only when it penetrates to the highest, first, necessary being, which can be an object to the reason alone. Why? Because with the conception of this being it first completes itself, because only in the idea of the highest nature is the highest nature of reason existent, the highest step of the thinking power attained; and it is a general truth, that we feel a blank, a void, a want in ourselves, and are consequently unhappy and unsatisfied, so long as we have not come to the last degree of a power, to the *quo nihil majus cogitari potest,* —so long as we cannot bring our inborn capacity for this or that art, this or that science, to the utmost proficiency. For only in the highest proficiency is art truly art; only in its highest degree is thought truly thought, reason. Only when thy thought is God, dost thou truly think, rigorously speaking; for only God is the realized, consummate, exhausted thinking power. Thus in conceiving God, man first conceives reason as it truly is, though by means of the imagination he conceives this divine nature as distinct from reason, because as a being affected by external things he is accustomed always to distinguish the object from the conception of it. And here he applies the same process to the conception of the reason, thus, for an existence in reason, in thought, substituting an existence in space and time, from which he had, nevertheless, previously abstracted it. God, as a metaphysical being, is the intelligence satisfied in itself, or rather, conversely, the intelligence satisfied in itself, thinking itself as the absolute being, is God as a metaphysical being.

---

mens fruitur, ut beata sit, tanquam summo bono suo. But is there any distinction here? Where my highest good is, is not there my nature also?

Hence all metaphysical predicates of God are *real* predicates only when they are recognised as belonging to thought, to intelligence, to the understanding.

The understanding is that which conditionates and coordinates all things, that which places all things in reciprocal dependence and connexion, because it is itself immediate and unconditioned; it inquires for the cause of all things, because it has its own ground and end in itself. Only that which itself is nothing deduced, nothing derived, can deduce and construct, can regard all besides itself as derived; just as only that which exists for its own sake can view and treat other things as means and instruments. The understanding is thus the original, primitive being. The understanding derives all things from God, as the first cause, it finds the world, without an intelligent cause, given over to senseless, aimless chance; that is, it finds only in itself, in its own nature, the efficient and the final cause of the world—the existence of the world is only then clear and comprehensible when it sees the explanation of that existence in the source of all clear and intelligible ideas, that is, in itself. The being that works with design, towards certain ends, that is, with understanding, is alone the being that to the understanding has immediate certitude, self-evidence. Hence that which of itself has no designs, no purpose, must have the cause of its existence in the design of another, and that an intelligent being. And thus the understanding posits its own nature as the causal, first, premundane existence: that is, being in rank the first, but in time the last, it makes itself the first in time also.

The understanding is to itself the criterion of all reality. That which is opposed to the understanding, that which is self-contradictory, is nothing; that which contradicts reason, contradicts God. For example, it is a contradiction of reason to connect with the idea of the highest reality the limitations of definite time and place; and hence reason denies these of God, as contradicting his nature. The reason can only believe in a God who is accordant with its own nature, in a God who is not beneath its own dignity, who on the contrary is a realization of its own nature: that is, the reason believes only in itself, in the absolute reality of its own nature. The reason is not dependent on God, but God on the reason. Even in the age of miracles and faith in authority, the understanding constitutes itself, at least formally, the criterion of divinity. God is all and can do all, it was said, by virtue of his omnipotence; but nevertheless he is nothing and he can do nothing which contradicts himself, that is, reason. Even omnipotence cannot do what is contrary to reason. Thus above the divine omnipotence stands the higher power of reason; above the nature of God the nature of the understanding, as the criterion of that which is to be affirmed and denied of God, the criterion of the positive and negative. Canst thou believe in a God who is an unreasonable and wicked being? No, indeed; but why not? Because it is in contradiction with thy understanding to accept a wicked and unreasonable being as divine. What then dost thou affirm, what is an object to thee, in God? Thy own understanding. God is thy highest idea, the supreme effort of thy understanding, thy highest power of thought. God is the sum of all realities, that is, the sum of all affirmations of the understanding. That which I recognise in the understanding as essential, I place in God as existent: God *is*, what the understanding thinks as the highest. But in what I perceive to be essential, is revealed the nature of my understanding, is shown the power of my thinking faculty.

Thus the understanding is the *ens realissimum*, the most real being of the old ontotheology. "Fundamentally," says ontotheology, "we cannot conceive God otherwise than by attributing to him without limit all the real qualities which we find in ourselves." [6] Our positive, essential qualities, our realities, are therefore the realities of God, but in us they exist with, in God without, limits. But what then withdraws the limits from the realities, what does away with the limits? The understanding. What according to this, is the nature conceived without limits, but the nature of the understanding releasing, abstracting itself from all limits? As thou thinkest God, such is thy thought; the measure of thy God is the measure of thy understanding. If thou conceivest God as limited, thy understanding is limited; if thou conceivest God as unlimited, thy understanding is unlimited. If, for example, thou conceivest God

[6] Kant *Vorles. über d. philos. Religionsl.* Leipzig. 1817. p. 39.

as a corporeal being, corporeality is the boundary, the limit of thy understanding, thou canst conceive nothing without a body; if on the contrary thou deniest corporeality of God, this is a corroboration and proof of the freedom of thy understanding from the limitation of corporeality. In the unlimited divine nature thou representest only thy unlimited understanding. And when thou declarest this unlimited being the ultimate essence, the highest being, thou sayest in reality nothing else than this: the *être suprême*, the highest being, is the understanding.

. . . .

GOD AS A MORAL BEING, OR LAW

God as God—the infinite, universal, nonanthropomorphic being of the understanding, has no more significance for religion than a fundamental general principle has for a special science; it is merely the ultimate point of support—as it were, the mathematical point, of religion. The consciousness of human limitation or nothingness which is united with the idea of this being, is by no means a religious consciousness; on the contrary, it characterizes sceptics, materialists, and pantheists. The belief in God—at least in the God of religion—is only lost where, as in scepticism, pantheism, and materialism, the belief in man is lost, at least in man such as he is presupposed in religion. As little then as religion has any influential belief in the nothingness of man,[7] so little has it any influential belief in that abstract being with which the consciousness of this nothingness is united. The vital elements of religion are those only which make man an object to man. To deny man, is to deny religion.

. . . .

Of all the attributes which the understanding assigns to God, that which in religion, and especially in the Christian religion, has

---

[7] In religion, the representation or expression of the nothingness of man before God, is the anger of God; for as the love of God is the affirmation, his anger is the negation of man. But even this anger is not taken in earnest. "God . . . is not really angry. He is not thoroughly in earnest even when we think that he is angry, and punishes."—Luther (T. viii. p. 208).

the pre-eminence, is moral perfection. But God as a morally perfect being is nothing else than the realized idea, the fulfilled law of morality, the moral nature of man posited as the absolute being; man's own nature, for the moral God requires man to be as He himself is: Be ye holy for I am holy; man's own conscience, for how could he otherwise tremble before the divine Being, accuse himself before him, and make him the judge of his inmost thoughts and feelings?

But the consciousness of the absolutely perfect moral nature, especially as an abstract being separate from man, leaves us cold and empty, because we feel the distance, the chasm between ourselves and this being; it is a dispiriting consciousness, for it is the consciousness of our personal nothingness, and of the kind which is the most acutely felt—moral nothingness. The consciousness of the divine omnipotence and eternity in opposition to my limitation in space and time does not afflict me: for omnipotence does not command me to be myself omnipotent, eternity, to be myself eternal. But I cannot have the idea of moral perfection without at the same time being conscious of it as a law for me. Moral perfection depends, at least for the moral consciousness, not on the nature, but on the will—it is a perfection of will, perfect will. I cannot conceive perfect will, the will which is in unison with law, which is itself law, without at the same time regarding it as an object of will, that is, as an obligation for myself. The conception of the morally perfect being, is no merely theoretical, inert conception, but a practical one, calling me to action, to imitation, throwing me into strife, into disunion with myself; for while it proclaims to me what I ought to be, it also tells me to my face, without any flattery, what I am not.[8] And religion renders this disunion all the more painful, all the more terrible, that it sets man's own nature before him as a separate nature, and moreover as a personal being, who hates and curses sinners, and excludes them from his grace, the source of all salvation and happiness.

[8] "That which, in our own judgment, derogates from our self-conceit, humiliates us. Thus the moral law inevitably humiliates every man, when he compares with it the sensual tendency of his nature."—Kant, *Kritik der prakt. Vernunft.* Fourth edition, p. 132.

Now, by what means does man deliver himself from this state of disunion between himself and the perfect being, from the painful consciousness of sin, from the distressing sense of his own nothingness? How does he blunt the fatal sting of sin? Only by this; that he is conscious of *love* as the highest, the absolute power and truth, that he regards the Divine Being not only as a law, as a moral being, as a being of the understanding; but also as a loving, tender, even subjective human being (that is, as having sympathy with individual man.)

The understanding judges only according to the stringency of law; the heart accommodates itself, is considerate, lenient, relenting, κατ ἄνθρωπον. No man is sufficient for the law which moral perfection sets before us; but for that reason, neither is the law sufficient for man, for the heart. The law condemns; the heart has compassion even on the sinner. The law affirms me only as an abstract being—love, as a real being. Love gives me the consciousness that I am a man; the law only the consciousness that I am a sinner, that I am worthless.[9] The law holds man in bondage; love makes him free.

Love is the middle term, the substantial bond, the principle of reconcilation between the perfect and the imperfect, the sinless and sinful being, the universal and the individual, the divine and the human. Love is God himself, and apart from it there is no God. Love makes man God, and God man. Love strengthens the weak, and weakens the strong, abases the high and raises the lowly, idealizes matter and materializes spirit. Love is the true unity of God and man, of spirit and nature. In love common nature is spirit, and the pre-eminent spirit is nature. Love is to deny spirit from the point of view of spirit, to deny matter from the point of view of matter. Love is materialism; immaterial love is a chimæra. In the longing of love after the distant object, the abstract idealist involuntarily confirms the truth of sensuousness. But love is also the idealism of nature, love is also spirit, *esprit*. Love alone makes the nightingale a songstress; love alone gives the plant its corolla. And what wonders does not love work in our social life! What

---

[9] *Omnes peccavimus. . . . Parricidae cum lege caeperunt et illis facinus poena monstravit.*—Seneca, "The law destroys us."—Luther (Th. xvi. s. 320).

faith, creed, opinion separates, love unites. Love even, humorously enough, identifies the high noblesse with the people. What the old mystics said of God, that he is the highest and yet the commonest being, applies in truth to love, and that not a visionary, imaginary love—no! a real love, a love which has flesh and blood, which vibrates as an almighty force through all living.

Yes, it applies only to the love which has flesh and blood, for only this can absolve from the sins which flesh and blood commit. A merely moral being cannot forgive what is contrary to the law of morality. That which denies the law, is denied by the law. The moral judge, who does not infuse human blood into his judgment, judges the sinner relentlessly, inexorably. Since, then, God is regarded as a sin-pardoning being, he is posited, not indeed as an unmoral, but as more than a moral being—in a word, as a human being. The negation or annulling of sin is the negation of abstract moral rectitude—the positing of love, mercy, sensuous life. Not abstract being—no! only sensuous, living beings, are merciful. Mercy is the *justice of sensuous life.*[10] Hence, God does not forgive the sins of men as the abstract God of the understanding, but as man, as the God made flesh, the visible God. God as man sins not, it is true, but he knows, he takes on himself, the sufferings, the wants, the needs of sensuous beings. The blood of Christ cleanses us from our sins in the eyes of God; it is only his human blood that makes God merciful, allays his anger; that is, our sins are forgiven us, because we are no abstract beings, but creatures of flesh and blood.[11]

[10] *"Das Rechtsgefühl der Sinnlichkeit."*
[11] "This, my God and Lord, has taken upon him my nature, flesh and blood such as I have, and has been tempted and has suffered in all things like me, but without sin; therefore he can have pity on my weakness.—*Hebrews* v. Luther (Th. xvi. s. 533). "The deeper we can bring Christ into the flesh the better."—(*Ibid.* s. 565). "God himself, when he is dealt with out of Christ, is a terrible God, for no consolation is found in him, but pure anger and disfavour."—(Th. xv. s. 298.)

Bibliographical Essay

There is a large amount of literature dealing with the topics discussed in this book. The following suggestions for further reading are very selective, but the reader who is interested in following up one of these topics will find interesting material here, and these works will in turn guide him to others.

A number of large anthologies have been published, including material on topics not found in this book. Some recent ones include G. L. ABERNETHY and T. A. LANGFORD, eds., *Philosophy of Religion: A Book of Readings* (New York: The Macmillan Company). W. P. ALSTON, ed., *Religious Belief and Philosophical Thought* (New York: Harcourt, Brace & World, Inc.). JOHN HICK, ed., *Classical and Contemporary Readings in the Philosophy of Religion* (Englewood Cliffs, N.J.: Prentice-Hall, Inc.), and G. I. MAVRODES and S. C. HACKETT, eds., *Problems and Perspectives in the Philosophy of Religion* (Boston, Mass.: Allyn & Bacon, Inc.).

There are also quite a few general works on the philosophy of religion. Some recent ones which discuss a set of standard topics are FREDERICK FERRE, *Basic Modern Philosophy of Religion* (New York: Charles Scribner's Sons), D. H. FREEMAN, *A Philosophical Study of Religion* (Nutley, N.J.: Presbyterian & Reformed Publishing Company), JOHN HICK, *Philosophy of Religion* (Englewood Cliffs, N.J.: Prentice-Hall, Inc.), and J. B. MAGEE, *Religion and*

Modern Man (New York: Harper & Row, Publishers). Hick's book is considerably shorter than the others. Magee's includes some material on oriental religions. On a more advanced level are JOHN HICK's *Faith and Knowledge* (New York: Cornell University Press) and ALVIN PLANTINGA's *God and Other Minds* (New York: Cornell University Press). Plantinga presents an unusually penetrating (though somewhat technical) analysis of several theistic and anti-theistic arguments and the problem of evil. Hick deals primarily with religious experience. GEORGE MAVRODES's *Belief in God: a Study in the Epistemology of Religion* (New York: Random House) discusses the general structure and role of argument, experience, revelation, and the problem of evil in theistic belief. A somewhat different treatment is that of E. A. BURTT, *Types of Religious Philosophy* (New York: Harper & Row, Publishers) which provides an excellent classification and discussion of several general approaches related to broader philosophical preferences. A. FLEW and A. MACINTYRE, *New Essays in Philosophical Theology* (New York: The Macmillan Company), is a collection of recent essays on various topics.

Turning specifically to the theistic arguments JACQUES MARITAIN's *Approaches to God* (New York: Harper & Row, Publishers), provides a brief restatement of Thomistic type arguments. There is a detailed discussion of them in ANTHONY KENNY, *The Five Ways.* C. S. LEWIS's *Mere Christianity* and *Miracles* (New York: The Macmillan Company), present some theistic arguments in an extremely readable form. Another presentation is in A. E. TAYLOR, *Does God Exist?* Somewhat heavier going is F. R. TENNANT's *Philosophical Theology,* Vol. II (Cambridge University Press) but it contains perhaps the most extensive twentieth-century presentation of a teleological type argument. ALVIN PLANTINGA, ed., *The Ontological Argument* (Garden City, N.Y.: Doubleday & Co., Inc.), is a collection of the most important ancient and modern discussions of its topic. C. D. BROAD's *Religion, Philosophy and Psychical Research* offers some brief but illuminating discussions and criticisms of several types of argument. The discussions in ANTONY FLEW, *God and Philosophy* (New York: Harcourt, Brace & World, Inc.), and BERTRAND RUSSELL, *Why I Am Not a Christian,*

(New York: Simon and Schuster, Inc.), are largely critical. As noted in the previous paragraph several of the works cited there include discussions of the theistic arguments.

On arguments against theism we have A. J. AYER's influential presentation of the positivist position and its application to theism in *Language, Truth and Logic* (New York: Dover Publications, Inc.), a position criticized by Plantinga in *God and Other Minds*. J. N. FINDLAY's "Can God's Existence Be Disproved?", in Flew and MacIntyre, *op. cit.*, is an attempt to reverse the ontological argument and disprove God's existence. E. H. MADDEN and P. H. HARE try to develop the problem of evil in *Evil and the Concept of God* (Springfield, Ill.: Charles C Thomas, Publisher), giving a verdict generally against theism, and so does Bertrand Russell, *op. cit.* JOHN HICK's *Evil and the God of Love* (New York: Harper & Row, Publishers), is devoted entirely to this topic, giving an extensive historical survey of approaches to this subject along with some original analysis. NELSON PIKE, ed., *God and Evil* (Englewood Cliffs, N.J.: Prentice-Hall, Inc.) is a collection of provocative essays, *pro* and *con*.

EVELYN UNDERHILL's *Mysticism* (New York: E. P. Dutton & Co., Inc.), provides an extensive discussion of mystical experience along with a valuable guide to the literature of mysticism. RUDOLF OTTO, *The Idea of the Holy*, is a penetrating account of the phenomenology of the kind of religious experience which tends toward the mystical. In *The Varieties of Religious Experience* (New York: New American Library, Inc.), WILLIAM JAMES gives a sympathetic description of many kinds of religious experience and adds his own tentative conclusions as to its significance in the last chapter. RONALD HEPBURN, *Christianity and Paradox*, and C. B. MARTIN, "A Religious Way of Knowing," in Flew and MacIntyre, *op. cit.*, criticize religious experience as a basis for belief. MARTIN's criticism is developed further in his *Religious Belief* (New York: Cornell University Press). C. D. Broad, *op. cit.*, includes a brief but helpful discussion of this topic, both *pro* and *con*, and the subject is treated extensively in MAVRODES's *Belief in God*, along with some attempt to reply to Martin's line of attack.

JOHN HICK examines voluntarism in *Faith and Knowledge*, as does Frederick Ferre, *op. cit.* James's "Will to Believe" is discussed in GEORGE MAVRODES, "James and Clifford on 'The Will to Believe'," in *The Personalist*, XLIV, No. 2 (Spring, 1963).

Two works presenting interesting alternative explanations of religious belief are MAURICE CORNFORTH's *Dialectical Materialism*, which gives a Marxist analysis, and SIGMUND FREUD's psychoanalytic account presented in *The Future of an Illusion.*